100
SIMPLE SECRETS
OF
SUCCESSFUL
PEOPLE

Also in this series

---

100 Simple Secrets of Great Relationships

100 Simple Secrets of Happy Families

100 Simple Secrets of Happy People

100 Simple Secrets of Healthy People

100 Simple Secrets of the Best Half of Life

Simple Secrets for Becoming Healthy, Wealthy, and Wise

100
SIMPLE SECRETS
OF
SUCCESSFUL
PEOPLE

WHAT SCIENTISTS HAVE LEARNED
AND HOW YOU CAN USE IT

DAVID NIVEN, Ph.D.

HarperSanFrancisco
A Division of HarperCollinsPublishers

HarperCollins books may be purchased for educational, business, or sales promotional use. For information please write: Special Markets Department, HarperCollins Publishers, 10 East 53rd Street, New York, NY 10022.

HarperCollins Web site: http://www.harpercollins.com

HarperCollins®, 📖®, and HarperSanFrancisco™
are trademarks of HarperCollins Publishers.

FIRST EDITION

Library of Congress Cataloging-in-Publication Data
Niven, David, Ph.D.
100 simple secrets of successful people : what scientists have
learned and how you can use it / David Niven.—1st ed.
p. cm.
Includes bibliographical references.
ISBN-13: 978-0-06-115793-6
ISBN-10: 0-06-115793-7
1. Success—Psychological aspects.   I. Title: One hundred simple
secrets of successful people.   II. Title.
BF637.S8 N58   2001
158—dc21   2001039538

06 07 08 09 10 CW 10 9 8 7 6 5 4 3 2 1

Contents

A Note to Readers   xi

Introduction   xiii

1 Competence Starts with Feeling Competent   1

2 It's Not How Hard You Try   3

3 Creativity Comes from Within   5

4 Take Small Victories   7

5 You Can't Force Yourself to Like Broccoli   9

6 Resist the Urge to Be Average   11

7 There Is Plenty of Time   13

8 It's Never Just One Thing   15

9 Don't Keep Fighting Your First Battle   17

10 Change Is Possible, Not Easy   19

11 Seek Input from Your Opposites   21

12 Write Down the Directions   23

13 Anticipate Irrationality   25

14 The Best Defense Is to Listen   27

15 Winners Are Made, Not Born   29

16 Do Things in Order   31

17 Get Experience Any Way You Can   33

18 Self-Motivation Works Once   35

19 Speak Slowly 37

20 Where You Stand Depends on Where You Look 38

21 Use Your Own Self-Interest 40

22 Remember Who You Are and Where You Are 42

23 Negotiate with Confidence, or Don't 44

24 Volunteer to Feel Better 46

25 Remember the Task, Forget the Rankings 48

26 Avoid the Second-Guess Paralysis 50

27 Seek a Tall Plateau, Not the Peak 52

28 Play the Odds 54

29 The Past Is Not the Future 56

30 Get a Good Night's Sleep 58

31 It Starts and Ends with You 60

32 Notice Patterns 62

33 Efficiency in Everything 64

34 Tomorrow Will Be a Better Day (But How Exactly?) 66

35 Lessons Can't Threaten 68

36 Success Is Formula, Not Fantasy 70

37 You Need to Know More Than
Just How Talented You Are 72

38 Role Models Are Not One-Size-Fits-All 74

39 Learn from Losses 76

40 Embrace Work; It May Have to Last Forever 78

41 Exercise and Eat Right 80

42 Boredom Is the Enemy 82

43 Be Clear About Your Role in the Outcome 84

44 Make Change Count 86

45 Listening Is More Than Not Talking 88

46 Take Off Your Blinders 90

47 You'll Get What You're Afraid Of 92

48 Think About Who You Ought to Be 94

49 Leadership Is Contagious 96

50 Want Support? Deserve It 97

51 You Will Give Up Faster if You're Not in Control 99

52 Life Is Not a Zero-Sum Game 101

53 You Don't Have to Get Straight A's Anymore 103

54 Whet Your Appetite for Success 105

55 Remember the Difference Between
You and Everybody Else 107

56 Your Work and Home Lives Must Fit Together 109

57 Nobody Wins Without a Loser 111

58 Tell Clean Jokes 113

59 Don't Want Everything 115

60 Look for Value 117

61 Get Your Motivation Where You Can Find It   119

62 Be an Expert   121

63 Failure Is Not Trying   123

64 You Are Not in This Alone   125

65 Your Goals Are a Living Thing   127

66 Avoid Roller-Coaster Emotions   129

67 Care   131

68 You Can't Be Persistent Without Perspective   133

69 Changing Jobs Doesn't Change You   135

70 It Might Get Worse Before It Gets Better   137

71 If You Don't Believe, No One Else Will   139

72 You'll Work Harder if You Feel Wanted   141

73 Don't Talk to Yourself   143

74 Seek Coherence and Congruence   145

75 If You Doubt, You're Out   147

76 Always Think About What's Next   149

77 Value Practical Knowledge   151

78 See the Risk in Doing Nothing   153

79 Face Conflict Head-On   155

80 Money Isn't Everything   157

81 Be Realistic About Yourself   159

82 Find Your Own Path   161

83 Own What You Do   163

84 Be Honest for Your Future   165

85 You Need to Know What You Are Looking For   167

86 Don't Forget Packaging   169

87 Learn to Lead Yourself   171

88 A Victory at All Costs Is Not a Victory   173

89 People Who Have It Right Work
Harder to Make It Better   175

90 Don't Run in the Wrong Direction Just
Because You're Near the Finish Line   177

91 Hope Springs Internal   179

92 Think as if Others Can Read Your Mind   181

93 You'll Get Knocked Down and Then Get Back Up   183

94 Keep Your Goals Where You Can See Them   185

95 Don't Settle   187

96 What Is the Point?   189

97 Win Your Own Respect First   191

98 Your Goals Must Engage All of You   193

99 Take Action   195

100 Only You Can Say if This Is a World You Can Succeed In   197

Sources   199

Acknowledgments   213

A Note to Readers

Each of the 100 entries presented here is based on the research conclusions of scientists studying success. Each entry contains a key research finding, complemented by advice and an example that follow from the finding. The research conclusions presented in each entry are based on a meta-analysis of research on success, which means that each conclusion is derived from the work of multiple researchers studying the same topic. To enable the reader to find further information on each topic, a reference to a supporting study is included in each entry, and a bibliography of recent work on success has also been provided.

Introduction

We gathered once a week for Professor Brian Lang's seminar. The topic was a little hard to define, but the purpose was to prepare us for the required yearlong senior research papers we would begin working on during the following semester.

All of us were writing papers on topics in our own majors, and among the twenty students in the course nineteen different majors were represented. One student was studying the civil rights record of the Johnson Administration, another the effects of lengthening the school-day for elementary students, another the question of whether a computer could be taught to write a song.

Although the course was meant to help us pursue our chosen interest, it wasn't about any one of them in particular. We were given no new information about Lyndon Johnson, no lectures on the attention span of seven-year-olds.

Instead, the course was about the process of undertaking a journey. While each of us was heading off in a different direction, Professor Lang hoped we would all reach the same destination.

The course explored themes of persistence and commitment and the unexpected discoveries that might be made along the way. "No outcome, no discovery, is really an accident; it is the product of the effort invested in the process," Professor Lang would say.

We continued to meet while we were researching and writing our projects. During class, the professor would ask each of us about our progress, what had excited or interested us, and what roadblocks we'd encountered. Nearly all of us would recount with excitement the latest new idea we'd been struck by or the indispensable book we'd just read.

One student would usually hem and haw and try to avoid making any kind of progress report. Eventually Professor Lang insisted he give us a full update, and he instead admitted he really hadn't been able to work consistently on the project. The professor's face was full of disappointment.

The student defiantly offered, "But you don't understand! I've got work coming out of my rear end."

"Have you had a doctor look at that?" Professor Lang asked.

The rest of us had been caught up in the tension of the moment and were then overwhelmed with laughter. But it was no laughing matter to Professor Lang, for he had no tolerance for not trying.

"Knowledge isn't going to track you down and force itself upon you," he had told us more than once.

For him, these research projects were a chance not only to learn intensely about the subject we had chosen, but also to learn about ourselves—to commit ourselves to a considerable task and to deal with the good and the bad, the discoveries and the setbacks. Professor Lang didn't really care if we could prove a computer could write a song or that twenty minutes tacked onto a schoolday would make kids better at fractions, but he cared passionately that we give our projects everything we were capable of, because if we could do that now, we could do it for the rest of our lives. And if we did so, we would succeed.

After the class stopped laughing at the doctor joke, Brian Lang turned reflective. He said, both to the slacking student and the rest of us, "What can any person do in the face of all the world's challenges? He or she can try."

As I conducted the research for this book, combing through thousands of studies on successful people, I thought often about Professor

Lang's course. Just as Professor Lang saw common elements necessary to creating a good research project, no matter what the topic, scientists have uncovered a set of practices, principles, and beliefs that are necessary for success, no matter what your goals in life are.

The *100 Simple Secrets of Successful People* presents the conclusions of scientists who have studied success in all walks of life. Each entry presents the core scientific finding, a real-world example of the principle, and the basic advice you should follow to increase your chances of success in your life.

100
SIMPLE SECRETS
OF
SUCCESSFUL
PEOPLE

Competence Starts with Feeling Competent

How good are you at what you do? Do you have tests or periodic evaluations or some other means to measure your performance? Surely, there is an objective way to demonstrate whether you are good at what you do and whether you should consider yourself a success.

Actually, people who do not think they are good at what they do—who do not think they are capable of success or leadership—do not change their opinion even when they are presented with indicators of success. Instead, their self-doubts overrule evidence to the contrary.

Don't wait for your next evaluation to improve your judgment of yourself, because feelings are not dependent on facts—and feelings of competence actually start with the feelings and then produce the competence.

ROSS, A DANCER from Springfield, Missouri, dreams of making it to Broadway. His road to dancing glory began with local amateur productions, the kinds of productions in which auditions take place in front of all the other performers trying out. Ross found the experience daunting; it was like being examined by a doctor with all your peers watching. "I was so scared. I felt like I had just come out of the cornfields," Ross said.

Sometimes he succeeded, and sometimes he didn't, but Ross was able to try out for different parts in various productions and gain tremendously from the experience. "I have more confidence about my auditioning technique now that I have done it in front of so many people so many times."

When he tried out for the first time for a professional touring company, he won a spot in a production of *Footloose*.

Ross has one explanation for his immediate success in landing a professional part: "I had confidence. If you want to do it, you have to really want it and believe in it. You have to make it happen. You can't sit back and hope that someone is going to help you along."

For most people studied, the first step toward improving their job performance had nothing to do with the job itself but instead with improving how they felt about themselves. In fact, for eight in ten people, self-image matters more in how they rate their job performance than does their actual job performance. (Gribble 2000)

It's Not How Hard You Try

Work hard and you will be rewarded. It sounds simple.

But remember what it was like studying for a test? Some kids studied forever and did poorly. Some studied hardly at all and made great grades.

You can spend incredible effort inefficiently and gain nothing. Or, you can spend modest efforts efficiently and be rewarded.

The purpose of what you do is to make progress, not just to expend yourself.

ACHENBACH'S PASTRIES WAS a Lancaster County, Pennsylvania, institution. The family-owned bakery had a loyal customer base and had operated profitably for more than four decades.

In the 1990s the owners decided to expand—to offer deli sandwiches and other goods and to add new locations for both retail and wholesale sales.

The bakery's owners had never worked harder in their lives than they did after the expansion. And in return for all their hard work, they got less money and the threat of bankruptcy because they could not keep up with debts incurred in the expansion.

Earl Hess, a retired business executive, provided capital to keep the company in business and then ultimately bought the entire operation. He looked at things as an objective observer and found that the bakery was doomed by inefficiencies. "They had too many products. Ninety percent of sales came from 10 percent of the products. They were losing their aprons making low-volume items."

Hess says when he took over the company he knew: "These people couldn't possibly have worked any harder, but they could have worked smarter."

Effort is the single most overrated trait in producing success. People rank it as the best predictor of success when in reality it is one of the least significant factors. Effort, by itself, is a terrible predictor of outcomes because inefficient effort is a tremendous source of discouragement, leaving people to conclude that they can never succeed since even expending maximum effort has not produced results. (Scherneck 1998)

Creativity Comes from Within

Everyone wants to think of something new—solve a problem no one else can solve, offer a valuable idea no else has conceived of. And every business wants to encourage its employees to have the next great idea.

So when a business offers its employees a bonus for creative ideas, a flood of great, original thoughts should come pouring in. Right?

We think that creativity, like any other task, can be bought and sold. But creativity is not the same as hard work and effort; it requires genuine inspiration. It is the product of a mind thoroughly intrigued by a question, a situation, a possibility.

Thus, creativity comes not in exchange for money or rewards but when we focus our attention on something because we want to.

JAPAN RAILWAYS EAST had the contract to build a bullet train between Tokyo and Nagano to be put in place in time for the 1998 Winter Olympics.

Unfortunately, tunnels built by the company through the mountains kept filling with water. The company brought in a team of engineers, who were highly paid to come up with the best solution. The engineers analyzed the problems and drew up an extensive set of plans to build an expensive drain and a system of aqueducts to divert the water out of the tunnels.

A thirsty maintenance worker one day came up with a different solution when he bent over and took a large swallow of the tunnel water. It tasted great, better than the bottled water he had in his lunch pail.

He told his boss they should bottle it and sell it as premium mineral water.

Thus was born Oshimizu bottled water, which the railroad sells from vending machines on its platforms and has expanded to selling by home delivery.

A huge cost was transformed into a huge profit, all by looking at the situation differently.

Experiments offering money in exchange for creative solutions to problems find that monetary rewards are unrelated to the capacity of people to offer original ideas. Instead, creativity is most frequently the product of genuine interest in the problem and a belief that creativity will be personally appreciated by superiors. (Cooper, Clasen, Silva-Jalonen, and Butler 1999)

Take Small Victories

Pursuing your goals is much like putting together a jigsaw puzzle. While you ultimately seek the final outcome, you still have to work piece by piece.

Since you will spend most of your time trying to make progress, you must enjoy what you are doing in order to finish.

Take joy from the process, and use the small successes to fuel your continued efforts.

LOUIS MINELLA SPENT a career planning every detail of the presentation of department stores. He knew everything about the business of catching the customer's eye and using the layout to maximize sales.

After thirty-one years in the business, he took early retirement. And then he looked for something worthwhile to do.

Louis decided to open a mailing center, where people can ship packages, buy boxes, make copies, and send faxes. It was a major adjustment. "I used to be just one member of the team in an international organization, but now I'm in charge of everything."

The hands-on difference was most significant. "Before, I was dealing with group managers. I used to issue reports and orders, but I didn't personally do the work or do anything other than tell other people what to do. I'm in reality now."

He takes great joy from the daily hurdles overcome, like adjusting the hours of his star sixty-six-year-old employee to keep her content or fixing the leaking ink in the postage meter machine or figuring out how to copy a seven-hundred-page document.

"It's a different ball game here, but it's tremendously satisfying to learn every little thing that your business needs."

Life satisfaction is 22 percent more likely for those with a steady stream of minor accomplishments than those who express interest only in major accomplishments. (Orlick 1998)

You Can't Force Yourself to Like Broccoli

Certain jobs require a distinct personality. There is little point in pursuing a job in communications if you are not an extroverted person who loves to interact with people. If your soul bursts with passionate creativity, you are not likely to be content with a job in accounting.

Personalities are like shoe sizes. They are not subject to our choice or preference, but they can be occasionally fudged—with uncomfortable consequences.

It is neither an accomplishment nor a fault to acknowledge that some people can speak before large audiences and be exhilarated by the experience while others would be petrified. Some people can study an equation for years and be fascinated by it, and others would long for human interaction and variety.

Realize who you are—what your true personality is—and choose a future that fits it.

HARDLY A DAY goes by without at least one of his clients refusing to work with him. In fact, sometimes they spit up on him. But photographer Jean Deer loves his job.

He has taken hundreds of children's portraits, and he is well acquainted with all the tricks of the trade to make a baby smile. Jean's an expert in every funny face and noise imaginable.

"When it's over, everyone—me, the parents, and the children—are exhausted, but that's usually a good sign."

Jean found that getting babies to flash their smiles wasn't the only way to get a great picture and that a grumpy baby was just another source of inspiration. "I was taking a photo once of this infant who literally wanted nothing to do with me. He would not look up, just stared at the floor." Jean got down on the floor with him, took the picture from a perspective he'd never used before, and wound up with one of the best pictures he'd ever taken.

The job requires two major traits, Jean believes. "Not everyone can just hang out a shingle and call himself a photographer. It's all a matter of being patient and energetic and then capturing the right moment."

Even as people experience different phases of their lives, including career and family changes, their underlying personality remains constant after about age sixteen. (Barto 1998)

Resist the Urge to Be Average

Everywhere around you are average people. They entice you into being more like them by offering their acceptance and by leading you to believe that everyone else is already more like them than like you.

But the "average person sales pitch" leaves out that you will be sacrificing your goals, individuality, and unique ideas and that you will lead a life determined more by the preferences of the group than by you.

"A PERSON WHO wants to be a leader must turn his back to the crowd," says the sign on Ty Underwood's desk. Ty runs a job placement service that works with laid-off and chronically underemployed workers.

"When I got here there was an attitude that this was all a show to keep the agency's funding. We'd show up, have the clients come in to fill out some papers, then send them on their way. Nobody behaving as if there was important work to be done, nobody behaving as if there was potential to be tapped here."

His first task was to change everything. To two-thirds of the staff, he minced no words: "Here's your resignation. Sign it."

Now each day begins with the premise that "Everyone who walks through this door can do more. That goes for the counselors and the clients."

Two years later, Ty has taken an office he considered an embarrassment and turned it into a model, with a job placement record of 71 percent.

Psychologists have observed that bad habits can spread through an office like a contagious disease. Employees tend to mirror the bad behaviors of their co-workers, with factors as diverse as low morale, poor working habits, and theft from the employer all rising based on the negative behavior of peers. (Greene 1999)

There Is Plenty of Time

W hatever our dreams are, we practically hear a clock ticking. Our family, our friends, even the media all make us wonder when we are finally going to be "there" and why we aren't there yet.

But there are no age restrictions on success. It takes as long as it takes, and when you reach it, you won't reject success because you're not the right age for it.

"THERE ARE PEOPLE on top, and then there are people who don't matter. That's how I felt," admits Nathan, who works in advertising in New York. "I looked down on myself for not being where I wanted to be, and I suffered through every day like it was my personal humiliation.

"I didn't take pride in what I did. I practically created a fictional job description for myself whenever anybody asked me what I really did."

Nathan says that in his business, "there's nothing but perception. We don't make better mousetraps, we don't make anything. We sell perception, and our jobs are perception. It was like I heard this clock ticking, with each day bringing me closer to failure."

Nathan sought help from a career coach who asked him who he was really competing with and why. "When I said I guess I was competing with everybody in the company because I wanted to be on top, she said, 'Well, if you were on top of the company, then you'd be competing with every other company to be bigger than them.' Basically, she made me see that there was no way to win this contest and that I could either sit back and enjoy the ride or keep trying to race to a place I could never get to."

Nathan's perspective shifted. "Now I try to keep my focus on doing the best work I can, and I know that I'll get where I'm going when I get there."

Age is unrelated to people's commitment to their job and their level of job performance. (Tuuli and Karisalmi 1999)

It's Never Just One Thing

When we think of attaining success, we often think of achieving a specific goal. Whether it's landing a new account, getting a promotion, or being offered a certain salary, we think that with just one more achievement we will feel successful.

But people do not change their assessments of themselves following an achievement. People react to the larger picture.

When you land the account or get the promotion or a raise, the same nagging concerns that led you to think you desperately needed one more achievement will undermine the value you place on that achievement.

Ultimate success neither comes with nor rides on your next achievement. Feelings of success come with the whole of your efforts, your beliefs, your experiences, your life. Success is based on the total package, not the ribbon on the package.

THEY DON'T TRAVEL in private jets and limousines. There are no roadies to unpack their equipment. They make no outrageous demands for huge dressing rooms or pampered treatment.

The members of the band Rustic Overtones are just happy to play their alternative rock music in clubs across the country. And when they are finished playing for the night, they pack up everything themselves in their rusty van.

Rustic Overtones plays 250 shows a year, has had its music played on 200 radio stations, and has sold 34,000 copies of its CDs.

But the band doesn't have a contract with a major record company, and much of its pay for gigs is used to offset travel expenses.

Will they make it? Drummer Tony McNaboe and the rest of the band certainly hope so, but he explains, "If you don't enjoy every minute of this, then you're in the wrong business. We play for crowds, we play for each other, we'll find a street corner and play for people walking by. We love making music, and whether we get a big record contract and head-line a big sold-out show or not, we'll be making music."

An event may be crucial in the short term, but researchers find that people's enduring self-concept—their view of who they are and what they are capable of—is not tied to any single positive or negative event. Instead, a self-concept is composed of a combination of beliefs and feelings based on long-term experiences both at home and at work. (Black 1999)

Don't Keep Fighting Your First Battle

P eople absorb a tremendous amount of information and learn significant lessons from their earliest experiences. We begin our careers as almost empty notebooks, and as we progress our mind fills with notations and observations. The first pages of our mental notebook are filled with our first experiences.

The potential for difficulty arises, however, as we try to apply those early lessons to situations in which they are not relevant.

Take note of experience, but realize there are situations where your experiences no longer apply.

SCHWINN BICYCLE was the leader in the industry for a hundred years.

Edward Schwinn, the fourth generation of Schwinns in the business, took control in 1979. Thirteen years later, the bicycle company was on life support, having watched its market share fall by 60 percent.

Analysts attribute the decline of the company to a refusal to live in the present. Because it was family owned, and always had been, Edward Schwinn refused outside financing when the company began to show signs of weakness. Because Schwinn was *the name* in bicycles, Edward Schwinn refused to spend money on keeping the brand name in consumers' consciousness. Because Schwinn was always the kind of company that operated on a handshake and long-term commitment, Edward Schwinn agreed to outsource all their manufacturing to the same Chinese supplier, Giant Manufacturing, without adequately protecting Schwinn's long-term interests.

By the end, in 1992, Schwinn Bicycle was $75 million in debt and losing a million per month. No investor would come near the company until it could be picked up for next to nothing in a bankruptcy sale. Product recognition among children dropped to close to zero. And Giant Manufacturing ended its deal with Schwinn and began producing its own bicycles in plants originally paid for with Schwinn money.

The company declared bankruptcy, and the Schwinn family lost all control over the family's business. Edward Schwinn's explanation for the fall? "We are where we are." To which one family member responded, "Where we are is out of business because you were asleep at the wheel."

Research on financial managers finds that 95 percent display a particular commitment to sectors in which they experienced their first success. Ultimately, this tendency leads to missed buying opportunities in other segments of the market and unrealistic enthusiasm for their chosen sector. (Goltz 1999)

Change Is Possible, Not Easy

Commercials on TV tell you all the time that you can change yourself. In thirty seconds, the commercial actors can get smarter, thinner, prettier, richer. But this fantasy world only sets us up for a fall.

We hear about the possibilities for wonderful changes people can make in their lives, and we want to duplicate those results. When we try and are not quickly rewarded, we actually wind up feeling worse than we did before we started.

The problem is, of course, that change is possible, but it does not come immediately. Nobody wants to sell us on a program for change that will take years because of course no one would buy it. But it does take years to accomplish the most important changes.

When you entered the first grade, you didn't expect to learn a second language, algebra, and the history of the War of 1812 all in the first week. You began an education that took more than a decade and provided you with incredible positive change.

Positive change in your life will not be finished today, but it can start today.

CHARLIE'S JOB is about change. He is brought in to smooth the transition when one company acquires another. It has given him a special perspective on the subject of change.

"Companies have cultures—ways of doing things, ways of life for the employees. These cultures aren't easy to change. Sometimes these cultures hold companies back from doing what they are capable of, and sometimes they make it impossible for two separate businesses to merge and exist together."

What Charlie does is study the cultures of the companies with an eye toward protecting the future. "When you have a culture that is not serving the long-term needs of the company, it needs to be changed—but changed carefully. If you change things too drastically, or change the culture in a negative, threatening way, then there will be high turnover, and you won't have changed the culture as much as destroyed it.

"Healthy change is a long-term process, whether for a company or the people in it," Charlie says.

The decision to make a change offers wonderful feelings of control and optimism, but those are short-lived if the change is not accomplished. Repeated efforts at self-change, characterized by an expectation of an unrealistically high payoff in an unrealistically short time, actually reduce satisfaction with our lives by 40 percent. (Polivy and Herman 2000)

Seek Input from Your Opposites

There are starters and finishers. There are big-picture people and detail people. Some are great at conceiving plans but lose interest in following through on them, while others are tenacious in seeing a project through but ill suited to dreaming up the next idea.

You benefit when you involve people in your projects who have traits and perspective that are the opposite of yours.

DR. HOWARD MURAD is a Los Angeles–area dermatologist who concluded that many of his patients' concerns about appearance fell at the intersection of medicine and beauty care.

He believed no one in either business fully appreciated that potential. "I wanted to address the patient's concerns, and if that meant using a facialist instead of laser surgery, then that's what I'd do."

Dr. Murad says the important question is, "If you had no disease, would you really be healthy? The answer often is no. What you need to be healthy is a sense of well-being, a sense of the ability to function at your highest level."

Twenty years after merging health and beauty care, Dr. Murad's business selling cosmetic products and spa treatments brings in $60 million a year. But he says none of this would have been possible if not for the fact that "I'm open-minded, I look at things differently, and I bring in people who know things I don't."

Teams in the workplace composed of people with differing personalities are 14 percent more productive than teams composed of more compatible individuals. (Fisher, Macrosson, and Wong 1998)

Write Down the Directions

If you were taking a complicated route out of town, you would write down the directions.

But if you were considering the future path of your life, your goals, and what you needed to do to achieve them, you probably wouldn't write any of it down. Think of it—the most significant journey of your life, and you probably won't put a word of the directions on paper.

Writing down your plans, goals, and ideas makes them more real for you. Every step you take to define what you want and what you need to do to get it increases the chances that you will actually pursue these goals and someday achieve them.

HARRY IS A CAREER counselor who works with professionals from various fields who feel unfulfilled. Harry doesn't just ask them what they really want; he asks them, "What's your quest?" He explores with people not what they *want* to do but what they *need* to do.

Harry often finds people unprepared to answer his question. "You ask people what they really need to do, and it strikes most of them as a question they either haven't thought about or gave up thinking about a long time ago."

Harry suggests that his clients keep a journal because he believes that in their journal their true quest will come to light. "If you write down whatever comes to you, you will be able to see the patterns of your thoughts, discover things you didn't even know about yourself, and discover how you fit into your quest."

People who regularly keep a journal, or some kind of written record pertaining to their aspirations, are 32 percent more likely to feel like they are making progress in their lives. (Howatt 1999)

13

Anticipate Irrationality

We understand the nature of a problem, and we carefully contemplate an ideal solution. Everyone should see how great an idea it is, and there should be no opposition.

Unfortunately, we often assume everyone is rational all of the time. A good idea will be supported because it is a good idea.

Experience eventually teaches us that those around us will make irrational decisions, often born in fears that have no realistic basis. Be prepared to sell your ideas not only in response to legitimate questions but also to ill-conceived fears others might express.

WORLD-RENOWNED economist John Maynard Keynes used to explain what the stock market is really about by comparing it to a contest British newspapers used to run. Contestants were given dozens of pictures of women and asked to choose the six that other people would think are the most beautiful. The person whose answers most closely resembled the collective opinion of the other contestants was the winner.

Keynes said, "It is not a case of choosing those which, to the best of one's judgment, are really the prettiest, nor even those which average opinion genuinely thinks the prettiest. We have reached the third degree where we devote our intelligences to anticipating what average opinion expects the average opinion to be."

In this game or in the stock market, Keynes argued, the task wasn't to figure out what was rationally best or what other people would think was rationally the best. Instead, the game and the stock market reflect the beliefs, ridiculously flawed though they may be, of the average person anticipating what other average people might think.

Research on the hiring process shows that a fear-based concern, often of the consequences of hiring a person who is too talented, is a factor in more than 20 percent of hiring decisions, despite there being no strategic or rational basis for the decision. (Baker 2000)

14

The Best Defense Is to Listen

Nobody likes to be criticized. And to some extent, everyone displays some measure of defensiveness, the impulse to reject any and all criticisms by denying their validity or undermining the messenger.

Unfortunately, defensiveness does not serve you. It encourages you to ignore potentially useful feedback, which inhibits your ability to improve.

Know that you are capable, and show it. But do not fight criticism merely because you can.

ED MADE IT to the executive level—vice president of sales for a well-established communications company. A bad year in sales hit the company hard, and layoffs reached all the way to senior management personnel.

Ed found himself sending out resumes for the first time in twenty years.

What he experienced was all manner of rejection—from being completely ignored to being told he was overqualified for the position he applied for. "I could do some of these jobs in my sleep. I couldn't believe I was sitting in front of some pip-squeak in human resources needing their approval," Ed said.

"My friends were sympathetic, but they told me I needed a new attitude. Knowing I should have these jobs and then treating the process as if it was beneath me was not going to convince anyone I was the right person for the job.

"They were right, and until I got past what I felt like doing and began to see what I should be doing, I didn't get anywhere."

Ultimately Ed, and his new approach to things, landed a job—ironically, in human resources.

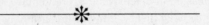

Defensiveness is negatively correlated with learning on the job. People with highly defensive personality traits speak more times in meetings, are more likely to interrupt a speaker, and are one-fourth slower in adapting to new tasks. (Haugen and Lund 1999)

15

Winners Are Made, Not Born

The great successes of our time are just extraordinary people on whom fate smiled, aren't they?

No, in reality, they're not. Successful people get where they are by following a strategic plan. They learn what it takes to get ahead.

We understand that to build a house it takes a plan, a blueprint, but we sometimes forget that to build a successful life, it also takes a blueprint.

CHEF WALTER POTENZA owns three thriving Italian restaurants in Rhode Island.

He studied and trained to be a chef, but he sees now that his abilities are the product of a lifetime education. When he opened his first restaurant, "All of a sudden my schooling, the knowledge and the history of my family, the respect and ethics of my father came into play. It made me an academic, a person who explored the food business."

And the learning never stops. "One of the secrets is, it's a business where you constantly need to stay on top. Chefs are not born." Walter explains that the process continues for him every day: "I'm an obsessive reader. Every time you read a book, you get ideas. Then you introduce your ideas into your workplace. You make more work for yourself, but you make that work better."

And success in the cooking business is something he has a clear definition of: "The success that I would like to have is to be remembered as a man who was innovative, who believed in authenticity and the culture of Italian cuisine in America. Food is the link to the past and to family. Success to me is not how much money you make. But if at the end of the day I was able to make fifteen or twenty customers happy, I'm a happy man."

Case study research on business executives reveals that 98 percent see their position as the result of plans and strategy and that more than half credit their use of a successful person as an example to help define that plan. (Gordon 1998)

16

Do Things in Order

I f you were making a sandwich, you would do it in order. First a slice of bread, then the fillings and seasonings, then the other slice. It wouldn't make sense to change the order. Even if you really liked mustard, you wouldn't put it on the plate first.

When we are pursuing our goals, however, we see the steps we want to take and sometimes try to skip the steps that are less exciting. But stepping out of order is ultimately frustrating and futile.

Take your goals one at a time, and appreciate the process as you move forward. Otherwise you won't.

JAMES MCINTYRE investigates airplane crashes. "At an accident, you see where things ended, and then you look backward to see how they began."

McIntyre, who grew up in poverty in the Bronx, trained to be a pilot in the Navy, went to college, and then had a career flying for the Navy and for commercial airlines.

He doesn't like to think very often about his childhood or his bumpy ride out of poverty. "Growing up in Fort Apache, I couldn't even imagine this life I've led. I had to live for the day because I didn't see much in tomorrow. The Navy brought me out of there and paid for college, but before I could think about the future, I had years of service obligated to them. The key for me was to do what I was doing well and not worry about what would come later. I knew that if I had proper training, I would be in great shape for the rest of my life."

Seven out of ten people who are satisfied with their careers express a strong sense of order—an appreciation for the different phases of a career and their progression to this point. (Elliott 1999)

17

Get Experience Any Way You Can

Take the first opportunity you have to get into the field of your dreams.

Even if the job itself is not what you want, you will get a better idea of what that line of work entails, and you will begin to prepare yourself for the job you ultimately desire. Or you might find out it's not the right job for you and that your future plans need to be adjusted.

FRED MARZOCCHI grew up with dreams of drawing for a living. "There aren't many ways to make a living with your sketchbook, but advertising was one of them."

When he couldn't find a job as a commercial artist, Fred became desperate for experience. He found a large drugstore chain with an in-house advertising unit and offered to work for literally nothing. They took him up on the offer, and within weeks not only had he gained professional experience, but the drugstore decided to pay him for his efforts.

After working for a number of advertising agencies, Fred went on to open his own graphics design and photography business. He often looks back on the offer to work without pay. "I just needed a chance, a start in this business, and I haven't had to work for free since," he says with a smile.

College students who served in internships were 15 percent more likely to find employment after graduation, and 70 percent believed they were better prepared for the workplace because of their internship experience. (Knouse, Tanner, and Harris 1999)

18

Self-Motivation Works Once

Declare something, say all the motivational speakers.

What do you want? Declare that you shall have it. Want to be in better shape? Declare that you shall be. Want to get a better job? Declare that you shall have one.

We are comforted, energized, enthused by these declarations. Our mood, self-image, and self-esteem improve.

Unfortunately, the effects are temporary and diminishing. When the outcome doesn't happen, we feel bad. And when we make our next declaration, it will be harder to work up even temporary enthusiasm as we recall the effects of our last failed plan.

Success comes not from self-motivating tricks and declarations of desired outcomes but from a steady, informed effort at progress.

WHEN DAVID CYNAR was hit by a car at age fifteen, doctors told him he might lose a leg. He thought his life was ruined.

As he looks back on the incident fifteen years later, David sees that the adversity may have saved his life. At the time he didn't care much about anyone or anything and had no motivation in school.

The accident took away his physical strength and made him look inward for new hope. "I became humbled at a second chance at life. But getting anywhere from there depended on self-confidence and self-worth."

Rehabilitation led him to study karate, and slowly he regained use of his leg and transformed himself not only into an athlete, but also into an intense and driven person. "Dedication and commitment have to come from inside you, but once you have them, you can go anywhere." Today, David juggles multiple passions as a successful salesman, a budding country musician, a black belt in karate, and a volunteer mentor for teens.

"I learned the hard way that positive thoughts and actions mean a healthier, happier, more successful life—and I love to share that with everyone I can."

For 87 percent of us, declarations of self-change produce a temporary improvement in self-image followed, in a few weeks, by disappointment, which makes our self-image worse than it was before the declaration. (Polivy and Herman 1999)

Speak Slowly

W̲e have a lot to say and only a short time in which to say it. The natural tendency is to try to pack in as much as we can.

But communication is not about the number of things we say, it's about the number of things that are understood. Good speakers master a practice that is simple but powerful: they speak more slowly than others.

NEWSMAN DAVID BRINKLEY'S distinctive delivery is known to generations.

He was a pioneer in network news, anchoring the original NBC news report before hosting the Sunday morning news analysis program *This Week*.

He credits a teacher's simple advice for a great deal of his success. "He said to me, 'The faster you speak, the less people will understand you. Take that to heart.' And I did."

People rate speakers who speak more slowly as being 38 percent more knowledgeable than speakers who speak more quickly. (Peterson, Cannito, and Brown 1995)

Where You Stand Depends on Where You Look

A re you doing well? Average? Below average? We know the answer. It's obvious, isn't it?

But how do you know the answer? Where does your response come from?

These judgments, in truth, are entirely relative. Feelings of success are based on our position relative to those who have accomplished less. Feelings of failure are based on our position relative to those who have accomplished more.

Your feelings are as dependent on your frame of reference as they are on anything you've done.

AS USUAL, Roger was out the front door and at his desk by 8:00 AM. The Cleveland area corporate accountant was in his twenty-fourth year with the same company.

Before lunchtime, he was called into the head of the division's office and told his services were no longer needed.

"When something like this happens, it really shakes you to your core. I don't care how prepared you are," Roger remembers.

The devastation was incredible, and denial followed. "This couldn't possibly be happening to me," Roger thought.

Roger read articles and books on dealing with layoffs and found stories of men who were so devastated by what had happened that they continued to dress and leave for work every morning, even though they no longer had a job, because they couldn't face telling their families or neighbors.

Roger began to see his situation in a different light. He still ached at the rejection he felt, but he realized that he had enjoyed more than two decades of reliable work, which had allowed him to prosper and provide for his family.

Doing some volunteer fund-raising work made him appreciate his situation all the more. "If you can't take some joy from all the opportunities and then steady yourself against the setbacks, take some time to think about the folks who have seen nothing but setbacks, and you'll realize all the good that lies ahead."

You might imagine that a promotion on the job automatically raises confidence and self-worth. Instead, studies find nearly half of recently promoted managers in the technology industry express uncertainty and doubt about themselves and their new position. Psychologists find that the promotion can undermine their self-confidence because instead of being the best among a group of lower-level workers, they now find themselves surrounded by more accomplished people to measure themselves against. (Cassirer and Reskin 2000)

21

Use Your Own Self-Interest

W hat is the difference between people who willingly take work home with them on the weekends and people who scoff at the idea?

What is the difference between people who work hard all day and people who do as little work as they can possibly get away with?

What is the difference between people who sign up for night school classes and those who can't imagine going back to school?

What is the difference between the most driven and the laziest person?

Self-interest.

We all do what we do because of self-interest; we think it's the best thing for us. Those who work hard do so because they believe there is a reward awaiting them that not only justifies their efforts but also demands their dedication. Those who do not expend themselves do so because they cannot see the long-term benefit of work outweighing the short-term benefit of laziness.

Remind yourself of the value of the things you want, and the costs to you in effort will not feel as great.

GWEN GOT HER start training dogs and soon realized she was really training their owners. "I would teach people about reacting consistently to what the dogs did so that good behavior was rewarded and bad behavior punished. And I thought to myself, it's not the dogs that are being inconsistent here, it's the people."

Gwen sees all kinds. "You have the gigglers who say, 'Isn't that cute,' when the puppy grabs their socks out of their hand and then get upset when the puppy goes for the socks, the shoes, the couch. You have the couples where one takes the strict approach and the other is in cahoots with the dog, covering up when the dog does something wrong.

"What dogs want," says Gwen, "is your love, attention, and treats. If you make it perfectly clear and consistent what it will take to get that reaction, your dog will behave because of self-interest. But it is also a matter of your self-interest," Gwen believes. "If you are too lazy to be consistent with your dog, or if you really don't care what happens to your socks and shoes, then your lack of interest will come across."

Researchers find that perceived self-interest, the rewards one believes are at stake, is the most significant factor in predicting dedication and satisfaction toward work. It accounts for about 75 percent of personal motivation toward accomplishment. (Dickinson 1999)

22

Remember Who You Are
and Where You Are

A big organization, by definition, must ask its people to put their own individuality aside and work as a group. There is little room for some of the aspects of your life that are most central to you, be they religious beliefs or cultural traditions.

The ability to put these things aside at the workplace is an asset to your organization because your beliefs and traditions no doubt would conflict with those of others, until nothing could be accomplished other than arguing over decorations and the relative superiority of ethnic foods.

Nevertheless, putting these things aside in the workplace does not mean putting them aside in your life. To feel we have succeeded in life, we cannot conclude we have given up the things that really matter to us. Otherwise, what have we really accomplished?

Those who express satisfaction with their accomplishments know that they can never toss aside the beliefs, customs, and values that they hold dear. They just display them on their own time.

BOBBY RICHARDSON played second base for the New York Yankees in the 1950s and '60s. Bobby went to work in an atmosphere that differed so much from his sheltered religious upbringing that he could hardly describe it to his family back home.

He knew that he had to keep his religion in his life, but he also knew that he couldn't bring it into the locker room or the dugout. That is why he helped found the Baseball Chapel.

Richardson's group met off the field and out of the limelight, bringing together teammates and players from opposing teams to share their faith.

Bobby explains: "You have to do something to make sure you aren't swallowed whole by the big leagues; then you'd never be the same again. But you can't impose who you are on everybody else, so the Baseball Chapel let me be a teammate on company time and be who I really was on my time."

Those who express the most satisfaction with their life and career tend to use a hybrid view of themselves. They see themselves as capable, team-oriented people on the job and as culturally and spiritually distinct people at home. Those who sacrifice their individual beliefs and backgrounds ultimately express one-third less satisfaction with their jobs and almost two-thirds less satisfaction with their lives. (Franklin and Mizell 1995)

23

Negotiate with Confidence, or Don't

You will face many negotiations in your life, whether for a pay raise or the terms of a car purchase. What determines whether a negotiation is successful?

Skill enters in. So does relative bargaining position.

But ultimately, when negotiations are prolonged, your willingness to continue is based on your level of self-confidence. No matter what your other advantages might be, you will end negotiations faster if you lack confidence, which means you'll settle for a less advantageous resolution.

ROBERT GOTTLIEB has spent a life working with writers, ultimately becoming editor of the *New Yorker* after a lifetime in publishing. His criticism is sought by renowned writers such as Joseph Heller and Toni Morrison.

He has negotiated everything about a piece of writing, from the payment to the punctuation. He even told Joseph Heller that *Catch-18* wasn't as good a title as Gottlieb's suggestion, *Catch-22*.

His theory of negotiating is simple: "If you're saying, 'Well, I don't know. Maybe. What do you think?' that's not helping. You have to be able to say what you believe in an unaggressive and uncontentious way. You have to believe it, then negotiate as if it were so. Whereas if you do not believe yourself, you cannot help. You have to be forceful."

Lower self-worth translates into 37 percent less willingness to negotiate and use of 11 percent fewer negotiation strategies. Increased self-worth correlates with greater willingness to incur the risks of prolonged negotiation and greater adaptability. In short, the less confidence you have in yourself, the faster you will give up trying to get what you want. (Greno-Malsch 1998)

24

Volunteer to Feel Better

You're busy. You don't feel there's much more you can do at work or at home. But you want to do more, and feel better doing it.

Take an hour this week and volunteer. Yes, give your time away.

Volunteering of course aids our community, but it also opens us up to a greater appreciation of our own lives, which enhances our motivation to do what we do the best that we can.

MICHELLE RUNS an office supply store in a Boston suburb. She works hard to keep the business thriving, and at the end of the day she needs a break. What does she do? She heads to the local YMCA, where she is a volunteer.

"It's challenging and exhilarating," Michelle says of her volunteer efforts to raise money to support Y programs. "I do it because I love it. I have been given a lot in this world and like to give a little back."

Even though she doesn't have a lot of free time, investing some of it in the Y actually makes Michelle feel better. "It reduces stress and gives me a real boost, because when you give time to a worthy cause you feel so good about yourself and the world in general."

Volunteers are 25 percent more satisfied with their jobs, have a better work ethic, and are more persistent in working toward long-term goals and rewards. (Johnson, Beebe, Mortimer, and Snyder 1998)

25

Remember the Task, Forget the Rankings

How would you react if everyone in your office was being taught a new procedure and you felt completely lost about how it worked?

Most people say they would hide their ignorance from their co-workers. This means that for most people, not letting anyone know they need help becomes more important than finding out what they need to know.

What is your true priority? Is it to cleverly trick your colleagues into believing you know everything? Or is it to learn what you need to know to do your job well?

PAT FLYNN RUNS a small manufacturing plant in northern Virginia. Pat tries to teach his employees the difference between style and substance.

"If everybody cared about style and not substance, nothing would get done. Why, we would never have had a man walk on the moon. There'd just be three guys jammed in the doorway of the spaceship, all trying to get out ahead of the others to get his picture on TV.

"The day we accept style over substance," Pat says, "is the day we stop making products that serve any purpose, that do any good. You want style over substance? Go do something that doesn't matter."

Researchers have found that a fascinating change takes place in school-children. When they begin their studies, strong and weak students show an equal willingness to ask questions when they do not understand. However, as they get older and begin to understand their relative position in the class, students, especially weaker students, become reluctant to ask questions and reveal what they do not know. (Butler 1999)

26

Avoid the Second-Guess Paralysis

We make decisions, even important decisions, all the time. All of us make the best decision possible given the information we have available.

But where do we go from there?

The satisfaction you experience from your decisions is based not just on the outcome of those decisions but also on the amount of time you consider counterfactual scenarios. What would have happened if I hadn't taken this job, if I had asked for a raise sooner, if I had pursued a different degree in school?

Because these questions invite you to think about an abstract world in which nothing is certain and every answer can be determined by your imagination, thinking this way can lead to an infinite series of what-ifs and could-have-beens. Just the act of spending time on counterfactuals can undermine the value of the decision you made in the first place.

What-if questions intrigue us—it can be endlessly fascinating to imagine what might be different—but what-ifs do not serve us or help us reach the best possible outcome for the decisions we have already made.

MIGUEL ARTETA'S FIRST taste of the movie-making business was unpleasant and intimidating.

"Because people would do anything to get their first movie made, there was this constant, spirit-crunching pressure. Every decision you made was made to please the potential backers, and then when they decided not to give you money for the project, you went back and thought about everything you changed to please them in the first place."

Then he came to the conclusion that the money chase was like a dog chasing his tail. "Everything was temporary until you got turned down, and then you started all over again."

Miguel decided that if he was really going to make his movie, it ought to be his movie. No more constant changes to attract backers. "We would take money only from people we respected, people whose opinions we felt good about."

Miguel wound up finding support for what became the critically acclaimed *Star Maps* and later said his movie came to life only when he "stopped second-guessing myself."

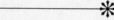

People who spend more time thinking about their possible selves, the lives they might be leading if they had made different decisions, are 46 percent less satisfied with their career decisions than people who do not spend much time imagining what might be different. (McGregor 1999)

27

Seek a Tall Plateau, Not the Peak

People on top want to stay on top. It's not surprising. But people who experience an incredible success wind up yearning for that experience long after it is gone.

Set your sights, not on reaching an ultimate moment that will quickly come and even more quickly go, but on reaching a level of achievement that is both satisfying and sustainable.

UPSTATE NEW YORK florist Patricia Woyshner has been in the business for forty years.

She's sold flowers to tens of thousands of folks in the area and even received one of the best assignments a florist could hope for—decorating the White House for the Christmas season. "I had to take a deep breath. I mean, you see pictures of the place all your life, then one day you're in the Oval Office."

Despite the excitement, Patricia's focus remained steady on her day-to-day concerns. "Doing the White House was exciting and rewarding, but my job is to run my business. I want to have something here that will last forever, that I can pass on to my children."

She realized that while she knew everything about flowers, she was not an expert in marketing her business. "All my education was related to the floral industry. I realized that I should try to learn from other industries because they face problems that are very similar to ours."

Patricia attended business school seminars designed to help her attract repeat business. Patricia reports the classes helped, her customer base is up, and even the White House called and asked her to decorate again.

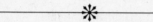

Studies of former Olympic athletes not surprisingly find that they are very capable and highly motivated individuals. However, more than half of former Olympic athletes have trouble adapting to more traditional post-athletic careers because they cannot replicate the heights of success and recognition they once enjoyed in athletics. (Sparkes 1998)

28

Play the Odds

There is an element of chance in everything.

Every aspect of your education and career has been affected by quirks of fate. Great jobs are found or ignored depending on who read the classifieds that day. New opportunities are glimpsed or missed depending on who is paying attention.

Still, you have to embrace the uncertainty of outcomes and realize that chance can play for you or against you on any given day. But the more you try, the greater your opportunity to benefit from a lucky outcome.

WHEN STEPHEN RETURNED from a weeklong vacation, there were 660 e-mail messages waiting for him. On an average day, he can barely handle all the messages that come in. "Keeping up? I am approaching the saturation point. There are moments of fear, of 'Good grief! How am I going to deal with all this?'"

He laments that e-mail has become the default communication tool for everybody, regardless of whether it makes any sense. "I get e-mail from people whose offices are three feet away." He doesn't like how it consumes time and affects the pace of his day. "You jump in and out of it like a conversation. It is incredibly damaging to productivity."

But, he says, if he turns the e-mail off, "I'm out of the loop. And that could be disastrous."

Instead Stephen has trained himself to sort through unimportant messages faster while ensuring that he doesn't miss the crucial ones. "You learn to multitask. I can now answer e-mail and talk on the phone at the same time, which is mildly ridiculous, but it means I'll see the one-in-a-thousand message I really need. It's a game of chance, but I have to keep playing."

Career analysts find that 83 percent of midcareer professionals believe chance played a significant role in their ultimate career path and that they highly value staying open for unexpected opportunities. (Williams, Soeprapto, Like, Touradji, Hess, and Hill 1998)

29

The Past Is Not the Future

I't's tempting to simplify things. The game is rigged. Some people have all the advantages, and they succeed. Some people have all the disadvantages, and they fail.

It is also, however, terribly misleading.

Your success is far more dependent on your behavior now than it is based upon where you grew up, where you went to school, or whether your path so far has been easy or difficult.

Opportunity lies ahead; it is a matter of whether or not you choose to pursue it.

JOHN PETERMAN HAD an idea to create a unique retail catalog and transform himself into J. Peterman.

Thirty-five investors in a row told him it was losing proposition. The thirty-sixth invested one million dollars.

His sales philosophy is based on awakening the imagination, because "your imagination is far more powerful than anything I could show you or tell you."

How did Peterman keep going in the face of so many rejections? "You fail a lot in life. Success is just overcoming failures." He compares the process of moving on after a failure to playing baseball. "If you think about your error, you'll make another error. Making mistakes is just a learning process."

Peterman's start down the road to success began with a childhood lived in modest circumstances. "By today's standards we were poor, but I didn't realize it." Instead he focused on what he did have: "I had ample opportunity to have nothing to do but cultivate a vivid imagination."

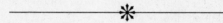

The current pattern of behavior employees engage in (both inside and outside the office) is six times more likely to predict job performance than is their background and job history. (Arrison 1998)

30

Get a Good Night's Sleep

When there are only so many hours in the day, and so much to do, the loser often ends up being sleep.

But sleep is a crucial factor in your ability to function. It is food for your brain.

You can sacrifice sleep to gain extra time, but ultimately you are sacrificing your ability to use your time with purpose and efficiency.

MATT SPENT years as a fitful sleeper.

"Most people know what it's like on Monday morning when you haven't had much sleep during the weekend. Well, imagine what it might be like when you haven't had enough sleep for five years."

Matt regularly felt sluggish. "My whole life was set in slow motion."

When he saw an ad for a research study on sleeping problems, Matt made an appointment, and the doctors asked him to sleep in the medical center for a few nights. They videotaped and monitored his attempts at sleep and found that a breathing problem was continually waking him up, making a full night's sleep impossible. The problem can be reduced or eliminated by wearing a special mask that regulates breathing while sleeping.

For Matt, the device has meant almost a whole new life. "I work better, I'm a better husband, I enjoy everything I do more."

Most Americans have been sleepy at their job, and two in five report making errors because of sleepiness. Inadequate sleep reduces innovative thinking by 60 percent and flexibility in decision making by 39 percent. (Harrison and Horne 1999)

31

It Starts and Ends with You

We live in a world where massive international corporations can grow bigger than a country. Yet many yearn for the freedom and personal responsibility of running their own operation. Given the number of different places the average person will work, the lifetime commitment of company to employee is a thing of the past.

Even if you never step out on your own, however, you will be making highly significant decisions about where you want to work and what you want to do. Accept personal responsibility for these decisions, and prepare yourself for the potential opportunities of the future.

"IF YOU HAVE the ability, believe in yourself, and can conceive it, then you have to have the determination to do it," says Dr. Bernard Harris, a veteran of multiple space shuttle flights and over four million miles of space travel.

Harris grew up in Gallup, an isolated village in New Mexico. But his dreams were limitless when he saw the Apollo missions on television. Before becoming an astronaut, Dr. Harris went to medical school and joined the Air Force as a flight surgeon.

"Nobody from Gallup has an easy path paved to success. You have to make your own way. And I never let anyone tell me I couldn't do something."

He frequently shares stories of his life with schoolchildren. He tells them there is only one way he could get the chance to fly in space: "Your attitude determines your altitude."

The ability to accept personal responsibility for work outcomes and to thrive under individual scrutiny improves your chances by 65 percent of successfully making the transition from working for a traditional large company to succeeding in a job at a small firm or as an independent consultant. (Peiperl and Baruch 1997)

32

Notice Patterns

What is the great common denominator of intellectual accomplishment? In math, science, economics, history, or any subject, the answer is the same: great thinkers notice patterns.

They see patterns no one else has thought of, patterns no one else has paid any attention to. Thinkers notice what goes along with what, and they consider the meaning behind those patterns.

Take time to consider patterns in your world that you've never thought about before.

"I DON'T CARE what you do, you have to understand how things work. Not just thinking about what you're doing, but about what you're not doing," says George Bodrock.

"Now my business is waste. It's not glamorous, but it's important. But what we're not doing enough of is finding natural techniques to reduce waste."

That's why George, of California's Ecology Farms, a commercial waste management company, researches "vermistabization." That's the process of using worms to transform waste into a useful product. Bodrock supervises the use of 160 million worms who eat their weight in yard waste every day and in the process convert the waste into a soil nutrient.

"It's the only real solution to the green waste problem. People are not going to give up growing lawns, gardens, and golf courses. We can take what they throw out and recycle it 100 percent."

Bodrock calls the worms' endless appetite for waste "the equivalent to a perpetual motion machine." He says, "We can build supercomputers that can do a billion calculations a second, but when it comes to breaking down green wastes, there's no computer to do the job. But we have to do it, and we have to keep looking for better ways. And when you do it right, you not only help the Earth, you'll become rich in the bargain."

Academic achievement, regardless of the subject matter, is characterized by an ability to decipher complex ideas and relationships. Experiments in language, math, and science show that the most basic building block of learning is independently observing patterns. (Silverman 1998)

33

Efficiency in Everything

E very organization suffers some waste. We've all heard stories of the federal government purchasing thousand-dollar hammers and hundred-dollar nails.

Sometimes we laugh at these matters, but ultimately they are very important to us. Nothing kills our initiative as quickly as the feeling that what we do doesn't matter. An organization that wastes important resources, like the efforts of its workers, is an organization that will waste your motivation.

"WELCOME TO the future of farming," says Rhode Island's Michael Lydon as he surveys his greenhouse.

Inside the quarter-acre facility, Michael grows as many tomatoes as the typical farm would produce on twenty times as much land. Other farmers "are very dependent on weather conditions. They are very dependent on water supply. They battle insects, they battle disease. They have to waste a lot of their time and money fixing problems they can't control. I have none of these problems."

Michael was an engineer before he began farming as a second career. And he looked at farming from an engineer's perspective, trying to root out waste and increase production. "Greenhouse farming is more about quality control, so my skills adapted very well to this business."

While the greenhouse is more productive than traditional farms during the growing season, Michael also benefits from a much longer season because his crops are protected from nighttime chills. For much of the year, his are the only local tomatoes on the produce store shelves. And unlike tomatoes that are picked before they ripen so that they don't spoil on the trip across country, Michael's tomatoes are picked when they ripen and taken straight to the markets.

Michael predicts the future of farming will be inside a greenhouse. "If you want to stay in farming, and consistently produce a product, your farming has to be done in a greenhouse."

Corporate inefficiency reduces job satisfaction by 21 percent and increases employees' desire to find new employment. (Melnarik 1999)

34

Tomorrow Will Be a Better Day
(But How Exactly?)

What do you want?

What do you need to do to get what you want?

What are your strengths, your weaknesses? What is the next step you need to take?

Forget about vague concepts and loose opinions. What are the facts?

Most of us have plans, lots of plans. And we have ideas, lots of ideas. But we so rarely turn our ideas into our plans, thus creating our future, because little of what we think about progresses beyond concepts and opinions.

Of course, we can never measure ourselves against concepts and opinions because they are too abstract to define. Thus, we can't say whether we're making progress or what we need to change.

Define your goals, and define your plans to attain them.

NANCY IS A CONSULTANT who works with small businesses. Her job is to help small business owners develop a map for their future.

She meets with her clients once a month to talk about where they are and where they are going. "Too many small business owners spend time dealing with one crisis after another rather than managing their business well. There's no time for thought, no time for progress, just time to do what has to be done today.

"The toughest hurdle," Nancy says, "is just getting started in setting concrete goals so that the business can serve the long-term needs of the owner rather than the owner spending all his or her time serving the short-term needs of the business."

People who construct their goals in concrete terms are 50 percent more likely to feel confident they will attain their goals and 32 percent more likely to feel in control of their lives. (Howatt 1999)

35

Lessons Can't Threaten

Try to teach someone who doesn't work with computers how much a computer might make their job easier. The most common reaction you find is stark reluctance. Why would anyone be against learning something that might make their job easier? Often it is because they fear that something that makes their job easier might one day take over their job.

Teaching is like asking someone to go on a trip. Just as no one is going to take you up on an invitation to travel on a trip from which they would never return, people will be reluctant to participate in learning about their own obsolescence.

When you try to teach anyone something new, you have to make it clear from the outset that the destination is someplace we'd all like to go.

"WHAT DO I need that for?" Jack protested when his granddaughter asked why he didn't use a computer. Jack had been a farmer all his life and had gotten along fine for fifty years without a computer.

His granddaughter gave him twenty examples of things he could do with a computer, such as keep track of his expenses or plan his growing schedule, and each time Jack replied that he been doing those things without a computer.

"What about the weather? What about reports you could get in an instant?"

Finally Jack relented, and a seventy-year-old farmer who had never so much as set his VCR was using a computer to track every aspect of his farm. Jack admitted old habits die hard. "I get stubborn, like anybody else. I don't need every newfangled thing to do this job, but every now and then a piece of equipment does help."

Feelings of self-threat are the single biggest obstacle in gaining the willing participation of workers in new training programs. Moreover, feelings of self-threat tend to spread among co-workers as they share their concerns. (Wiesenfeld, Raghuram, and Raghu 1999)

36

Success Is Formula, Not Fantasy

Watch a movie or a TV show, and see what makes people successful and happy. It's usually some almost magical quality or event.

In real life, the main difference between people who achieve and people who do not isn't as exciting or mysterious, but it is as important. It is simply conscientiousness. People who approach things with order, common sense, consistency, and persistence will ultimately succeed.

IN THE EARLY 1950s, Lillian Vernon spent five hundred dollars on her first advertisement. She offered monogrammed belts and handbags, and when she was finished filling the first round of orders, she had made thirty-two thousand dollars in profits.

From her first successful ad to fifty years later, Lillian Vernon has been selling household items and gifts and steadily expanding her sales. Her company now generates more than $250 million in sales every year and is one of the fifty largest companies owned by a woman in the United States.

Lillian met with her share of skeptics: "There were naysayers along the way, but I couldn't be defeated. Because all it really takes is commonsense intelligence and hard work." Which for the seventy-one-year-old businesswoman still means a six-day workweek.

In a study of recent business school graduates, employee conscientiousness was five times more likely to predict supervisor satisfaction than was employee intelligence. (Fallon, Avis, Kudisch, Gornet, and Frost 2000)

37

You Need to Know More Than Just How Talented You Are

Y ou need confidence to succeed. You've seen that, you've read that, you know it. But your self-esteem must be built on a foundation of self-respect.

All of us will suffer blows to our self-esteem when we fail. Regardless of how strong our beliefs are, negative outcomes will shake us.

That is why you must realize not just how capable you are, but who you are. When events undermine your self-esteem, you must have faith in yourself that is unquestionable, undeniable. This faith in your integrity and your humanity will survive any attack based on a failure or even a series of failures. It will give you something to start from as you rebuild your self-esteem.

PETER SHANE IS the dean of the University of Pittsburgh Law School. He tells his graduates that after learning the law, and even achieving confidence in themselves, their education is not complete. "You will need more. You will need courage, especially if you are going to be a leader in the settings where you live, work, and worship. If you advocate change, you will have to understand that there is no change so small that it threatens no one."

The dean tells students that the world is filled with temptations to "cut corners" and to take "the path of least resistance." To overcome, they must see their actions as examples for others. "There is no greater measure of the example you provide as a leader, as a lawyer, as a citizen, or as a parent than the decency with which you treat other human beings. This is true whether you're dealing with a friend or foe, colleague or opponent, superior or subordinate."

If they follow this path, Dean Shane tells them, "You will have the luxury of looking back on a life well lived."

Self-esteem, by itself, does not predict success. In fact, those with particularly high self-esteem are 26 percent more vulnerable to the consequences of failures and setbacks because of the devastating effect negative outcomes can have on their self-image. (Coover and Murphy 2000)

38

Role Models Are Not One-Size-Fits-All

We often see stories of inspiring people and wonderful successes. Some of us put their pictures on our walls or clip notable quotes from them. But what does that do for us if the inspiring person has done things we will never or could never do?

For many of us, the choice of a role model invites comparison, and if our abilities and outcomes do not measure up, the role model serves not as an inspiration but as a source of frustration and defeat.

Choose as your role model someone who has accomplished something you can accomplish and something you want to accomplish. There is tremendous value in using co-workers or family members whom you admire rather than famous athletes, leaders, or historical figures, who have experienced great successes but whose experience has less in common with yours.

HEIDI MILLER HAS served as the chief financial officer for the multinational financial giant Citigroup and later for the Internet sales business Priceline.com.

While she made her steady climb through the corporate world, each step brought her further into isolation. Her old friends dismissed the corporate calling: "You're going to work for a bank? You're such a traitor." Meanwhile, her colleagues were not terribly supportive. "I felt marginalized," Heidi lamented.

She knew that if she was having trouble finding the support she hoped for, no doubt many others like her were going through the same experience. That's why she founded Women and Company, an association of businesswomen who meet periodically to share their exploits and offer support and positive examples for one another. Heidi finds the group "fabulous because it is so reassuring."

People who actively target someone to serve as a role model draw positive feelings from that person only if the role model's achievements are both relevant and attainable. People who choose role models who do not fit that description wind up 22 percent less satisfied with their careers than people who do not have a role model at all. (Lockwood and Kunda 2000)

39

Learn from Losses

The setbacks you experience are wonderful opportunities to learn. Not only can you learn, in a critical sense, what you might have done wrong, but you also can come to understand what has led you to make the choices you've made.

Are you pursuing the goal you truly want? Are you pursuing a goal whose steps you are suited for? Practice gaining something every time things don't go your way.

IN COLLEGE, Mary Ann sweated through a pharmacy program, one of the most challenging majors available. She had her eye on a career that would pay well and perform a public service.

Only after graduating did she see the options that were truly available to pharmacists today. "Basically, you can sign on for life with a mega-pharmacy, working long hours in a windowless warehouse, slapping labels on bottles, and never seeing, much less talking to, your customers. Or, you can sign on for a small neighborhood operation that will either go out of business or be bought up by a superchain within six months."

Mary Ann opted for the mega-pharmacy and, not surprisingly, didn't enjoy her work.

After six years of very steady work, she and two colleagues began making plans to open their own store where they could work on their own terms and feel like they were helping people. "My desire for change overwhelmed my fears of what would happen out on our own," Mary Ann explained.

"I wasn't in the right place. I needed to make a change because I knew I was in the wrong job, and I began to worry I was in the wrong career. But I don't look at my decision as a disaster, because people often fail, but if they learn from failures, then they have gained something in the process."

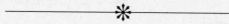

A majority of students who failed in college and later returned for their degree report that the biggest difference in their second chance was better knowledge of themselves and their capabilities and commitments. (Robeson 1998)

40

Embrace Work;
It May Have to Last Forever

We live in a culture that cherishes the dream of early success fol- lowed by early retirement. We read of a retirement utopia await- ing those who can afford it.

In truth, most retirees base their identity on their career and yearn for the activity and responsibility their work life provided.

FOR EIGHTY-ONE-YEAR-OLD Vincent, a lifelong New York resident, retirement after sixty years of work has not been a dream come true. "Some people seem so happy to be retired, but I feel lost. A sense of fulfillment is missing."

But by serving on the local community board, which makes deci- sions on zoning and land use, he has found a way to keep himself engaged. "The community board keeps me moving," Vincent says.

The board, which is unpaid, often has to deal with contentious issues pitting neighbor against neighbor. Vincent tries to help everyone stay calm, and he keeps his own comments to a minimum. "If I say something, it has to be worth saying." But when the time comes to take a vote, he calls on a lifetime of experience. "I've run more organizations than I now have hairs on my head. I think, 'What did I do then?' That helps."

The single biggest factor in shaping a retired person's identity is career history, outweighing even family life. (Szinovacz and DeViney 1999)

41

Exercise and Eat Right

You're focused. You use your time well so that you can accomplish as much as possible. Because you're busy, you don't have time to exercise, and you grab some fast food because it's quicker.

That makes about as much sense as trying to save time by never buying gasoline, then having to walk to work when the car dies.

Healthy habits increase our energy and improve both our performance and our satisfaction on the job. It may take more time, but in the end, preserving your own health makes possible everything else you want to do.

KATHRYN HAS a time-consuming, demanding job in a major accounting firm. "With that lifestyle, you are constantly under stress working with Fortune 500 companies who want what they want when they want it. Exercise, eating right—those were things I hadn't had time for in twenty years."

Her doctors advised her that her health was at risk. She listened.

Gone were the high-fat fast foods, and in place of an extra hour of work when she got home was an hour of walking.

The results have been fantastic. "I don't know when I've felt so good," Kathryn says. She not only feels better, she also works better now. "I'm more levelheaded. There's still a lot to do, but I don't feel like I have to knock anybody out of my way to do it."

Comparing middle management employees, researchers have found that those whose careers continue to have momentum are 53 percent more likely to engage in healthy life habits than those whose careers are stalled. (Roberts and Friend 1998)

42

Boredom Is the Enemy

B oredom will eat away at your persistence and resolve. No one can do the same job, requiring the same tasks, with perpetual interest and enthusiasm.

When evaluating a job opportunity, don't just worry about the salary and workload; investigate how much variety there is in the tasks you'll perform.

LOREN SCHULTZ has spent forty-five years running companies and riding the wave of technology in data management.

Some of his ideas have worked spectacularly well, and some have fizzled out, overtaken by something better. "Everything we've done is based on someone having a new idea and pursuing it," Loren says.

He no longer starts companies from scratch. Rather, he now uses his vast experience to run a business incubator, which provides office space, consulting, and capital to new businesses. What Loren loves is taking everything he's learned and using it to help newborn companies grow. "Every day is a different adventure. I'm like the grandfather around here. I'm not in charge of anything, but I'm available to talk about anything. I've got a lot of experience, so why not share it with people? And the best part of working with all these different companies is, it's fun."

Low-variety jobs produce twice as much employee turnover and three times less job satisfaction than high-variety jobs. (Melnarik 1999)

43

Be Clear About Your Role
in the Outcome

President Kennedy was fond of a quote from Confucius: "Victory has a thousand fathers; defeat is an orphan." We tend to take credit for successes while spreading the blame for failure on the shortcomings of others.

We need to be clear about our own role in the outcome, whatever it is. If we overstate our own role in a success, we will be ill prepared to repeat the things that actually produced the success. Similarly, if we ignore our own role in an unsuccessful effort, we will fail to think about and learn from our own mistakes.

It is comforting to think about everything that goes right as being a product of our personal abilities and everything that goes wrong as being the fault of others. But it is not useful to us because it will not help us produce future successes.

MANY PEOPLE CONSIDER Paul Baran the "father of the Internet." Paul was an engineer for the Rand Corporation in the 1960s and played a major role in conceiving the packet switching process that became central to the development of the Internet.

Paul, who emigrated to the United States from Poland when he was a small child, tried to sell his conception of the Internet to major communication companies. They were uniformly uninterested. He recalls executives dismissing him immediately. "Imagine them listening to this young guy and saying, 'Listen, now, squirt . . .'"

Paul did not give up on himself or his idea and instead realized that what he needed was not a different product or sales pitch but a different audience.

He found his audience when he presented his ideas to the U.S. military, where the potential for what he was offering was appreciated.

Paul is quick to share the credit for his efforts. "The Internet represents the work of thousands of people. Each of us had a little piece." And thirty years after he helped get the Internet off the ground, he's still dreaming up big ideas that turn into profitable operations: "I start these companies, then I find somebody smarter than myself to run them, and I get the hell out of the way."

When people are asked to attribute successes and failures, to explain how things happened, they are seven times as likely to focus on the significance of their efforts when describing a success as they are when describing a failure. This tendency is 19 percent greater among less experienced workers, who take more credit for successes and dish out more blame for failures—and learn nothing in the process. (Moeller and Koeller 2000)

44

Make Change Count

We are all tempted by change. Whether it's a change in procedure or a change in jobs, we are hit with a wave of enthusiasm as we focus on the potentially positive results.

All talented people want to make changes in their lives and in the world around them. If you believe you are talented, you begin with the notion that you can do things better, and therefore you should.

But it makes no more sense to rush into making every change you can than it does to run away from every change possible.

"I'VE TRIED to go in so many directions, I don't know where I am anymore. I've tried so many programs, I've lost count," says Teresa, a paralegal in Charlotte. "Now I need a program for people who've tried too many programs."

She describes the cycle: "I fall for the sales pitch, I jump in, and then a short time later I don't feel like it's working. Then the cycle starts all over again."

Finally one of her friends gave her some advice. "She told me that I have to approach changing my life more like I'm buying a house than like I'm buying a dress. It's not permanent and irreparable, but it ought to reflect serious consideration and a solid commitment."

Says Teresa, "In a way, it's a good thing all these programs didn't work, because I've signed up for so many, I'd be fifty-six different people by now if they'd worked."

People who rate themselves as intelligent have a 47 percent higher need for change in their professional world. They regularly see possibilities and opportunities around them but must be wary of allowing boredom to encourage them to pursue change for the sake of change. (Whatley 1998)

45

Listening Is More Than Not Talking

We think about what we have to say, how much to say, and how best to say it. We invest so much in talking that we sometimes treat the time when we're not talking as a rest break.

Instead, active listening, investing ourselves in what others are saying, is the only way we can learn from others and adapt what we have to say to correspond to the other person's perspective.

DON HAS BEEN married for forty-seven years. He admits not everyone saw his potential for being a good husband. "My own mother used to wonder how my wife put up with me. If I ever told her about a disagreement we'd had, she would tell me to turn right around and apologize. Every time."

He continues, "One time, while I wasn't paying very close attention, my wife told me an interesting story about a neighbor. The next day I repeated the story to her, forgetting that she had been the one who told me."

Before too long, Don began to understand the importance of communication in their arguments. "We would argue about one person not doing what they agreed to do or forgetting something important, and it became clear that the problem was we weren't paying enough attention in the first place."

Don says now, "I realized that listening is a skill, and like any other skill, the less attention you give to it, the more mistakes you make. Only these are mistakes you can't cover up, because the person who was talking to you knows you made them."

Good talkers tend not to be good listeners. Indeed, people who think of themselves as good talkers tend to rate themselves as extroverted, while good listeners rate themselves as introverted. Good listeners are 60 percent more likely to try to put themselves in the other person's place—trying to see things through their perspective. (Pauk 1997)

46

Take Off Your Blinders

Perspective is a powerful force. From a young age we are taught to hold certain expectations, and those expectations influence how we see the world.

Stereotypes inculcated in you when you were a child may be affecting how you evaluate other people and even how you evaluate yourself.

Nobody rationally chooses to limit their aspirations, deny themselves opportunities, and misjudge other people's talents based on a set of stereotypes. But that is just what we do without even thinking about it because stereotypes alter our view of the world.

IN RURAL NORTHERN New Hampshire, the Women's Rural Entrepreneurial Network (WREN) is helping hundreds of women make an income from their homes. WREN's members run the gamut from women selling hand-made crafts in their spare time to women offering professional services such as graphic arts design and bookkeeping full-time.

WREN's director, Natalie Woodroofe, says the group helps bring together women who otherwise might be isolated and lonely and feel there are no opportunities available to them. The members feel empowered to succeed and are more likely to overcome the skepticism that rural women working from home face when they try to make a living. "These women get more than their share of discouragement from people who act like they are seven-year-olds selling lemonade in their front yard."

Instead, WREN connects these work-at-home women with a network of women of all ages and professions. "There are attorneys and traditional business managers or owners who donate their time to WREN, and these two very different women can greet each other on the street and feel a bond. WREN crosses all those barriers—economic, cultural, educational—so that women can see their capabilities and their connections with each other."

Natalie says, "Women who are creating and supporting themselves should feel good about what they do, and WREN helps make that happen."

People who are prone to use stereotypes in assessing themselves and others are 39 percent more likely to believe that opportunities are limited for others and themselves. (Frome 1999)

47

You'll Get What You're Afraid Of

When we spend time worrying about things that could go wrong, we're not spending time trying to improve. Which means that worrying about things going wrong increases the chances that they will go wrong.

Accepting that sometimes we will succeed and sometimes fail frees us to pursue achievements and to spend time thinking about what we can do instead of what we can't.

"MOST BUSINESS is built on a foundation of rejection. If a business hired everyone who applied for its jobs or bought every product a sales rep offered it, then it would be bankrupt in ten minutes," says Martin, an acting coach who has counseled hundreds of budding thespians.

"Unless you don't want anything, you'll have to learn how to love rejection, because it will be coming." He points to the acting business for ample evidence. "There isn't an actor you've heard of—there isn't an actor alive—who hasn't been rejected for more parts than they'll ever get.

"It doesn't mean that you love to lose," Martin believes, "but that you embrace the process that gets you to the outcome you want. And rejection is just a step in the process."

In a survey of high-tech employees, those who spend "a lot" of time worrying about their jobs are 17 percent less productive than workers who "seldom" or "never" worry about their job. (Verbeke and Bagozzi 2000)

48

Think About Who You Ought to Be

I f you could snap your fingers and change anything about yourself and your life, what would you change?

Did you ask for riches and fame? Or did you ask for industriousness, caring, and honesty?

The more you direct yourself toward a fantasy life, the less satisfied you will be with who you are and the more frustrated you will become as you fail to attain the fantasy. The more you direct yourself toward a better, more fulfilling life, the more you can actually lead a better, more fulfilling life.

LISA WORKS in communications and thinks of herself as the second Darren on the old television show *Bewitched*. Every day there is a different person doing her job, and no one seems to notice.

Lisa works every other day in a job-sharing plan, while her partner at the company takes the other days. Lisa asked for the arrangement to spend more time with her child, but she recognizes the challenge of the shared job. "It's a relay race, while most of us are used to running by ourselves. It requires tremendous cooperation, organization, and mutual respect."

Although thrilled when her boss approved the work-sharing plan, Lisa acknowledges, "Every fantasy has a reality. The choice comes down to time or money, and you have to make a decision which matters more."

Cutting her salary has made things a little tight at home, and she is concerned her potential for advancement may be hurt when she returns to working full-time, but for her the decision was clearly the right thing to do. "I have a healthier perspective on life and a healthier family life, and nothing matters more to me than that."

People who are focused on the "ideal" life they could lead are 34 percent more likely to be anxious and self-conscious about their lives, while people focused on the life they "ought" to lead are more caring about other people in their lives and actually 21 percent more oriented toward achieving in their career. (Bybee, Luthar, and Zigler 1997)

Leadership Is Contagious

True leadership strengthens the followers. It is a process of teaching, setting an example, and empowering others.

If you seek to lead, your ability will ultimately be measured in the successes of those around you.

"THIS ISN'T a job for individuals working alone; this is a job for a team," says police chief Frank Blane, who directs a department of one hundred officers in central California. "I look at it as being a conductor of an orchestra, trying to make sure everyone is in tune."

Chief Blane sets the direction of the department in everything he does. "You have to be very, very fair to the officers, and then they get the message that they have to be that way to every citizen they interact with."

Blane adds, "The way chiefs get in trouble is showing favoritism. When the top goes bad, then the rest of the organization goes bad. But when the top sets the right tone, then everybody can follow that lead."

Despite the power we associate with the idea of a leader, 93 percent of those who actually lead an organization view themselves at least partially as a servant of the people in their organization. (Boyer 1999)

Want Support? Deserve It

When someone in the office gets promoted, will colleagues offer support and sincere congratulations, or will they snipe and complain?

The difference comes down to whether they think the promotion was deserved.

To maintain the support of your co-workers as you advance, you have to let them see how hard you are working long before the promotion as well as after it. You have to let them see how capable and dedicated you are. You will maintain far more support from co-workers for appearing overly dedicated to your work than you would receiving a promotion they do not feel is justified.

STERLING AND SHANNON Sharpe grew up playing football together on the farm in Glenville, Georgia.

Sterling, the older brother, was recruited by a football powerhouse, the University of South Carolina, and went on to become a first-round draft pick in the National Football League. Shannon was not heavily recruited and wound up playing football in obscurity at Savannah State College, before fighting his way onto an NFL roster as the last man drafted by the Denver Broncos in 1990.

Sterling was among the league's best wide receivers, trying desperately to help his team to the Super Bowl, when a neck injury cut short his career. Shannon's skills continued to develop, until he too became recognized as one of the premier pass catchers in the game.

Shannon's Denver Broncos made it to two consecutive Super Bowls, and then he won a third Super Bowl as a member of the Baltimore Ravens. When Sterling was asked whether he was jealous of his brother's continued success and Super Bowl rings he said, "It's very easy to pull for him because I know what this means for him and I know how hard he worked to get there. The same goals and dreams and work ethic and everything Shannon put into getting there, I experienced as a player trying to get there myself."

Over eight in ten people will support their friends moving up beyond them, even support the advancement of peers who they are not friendly with, if they feel the promotion was based on achievements and ability. (Feather 1999)

51

You Will Give Up Faster if You're Not in Control

Some people give up the moment an obstacle is placed in front of them. Some people doggedly continue to pursue a goal even after years of frustration and failure.

What is the main difference between these people? It's not ability or even patience. It is actually their sense of control.

Those who feel they are not responsible for choosing their goals and pursuing them tend to believe that results are arbitrary. To them, it doesn't matter how hard you try or how talented you are, being successful is like winning the lottery; it's all a matter of luck. With this attitude, it hardly makes sense to work hard or be dedicated to a dream or goal.

Those who persevere, conversely, recognize that they are ultimately responsible, not just for pursuing their goals, but for setting them. When you are in control, what you do matters, and giving up will not seem very attractive.

DARNELL ELLIS, a blues guitar man, once played alongside musical legend B. B. King. Then alcohol addiction brought on a series of troubles in his life. When circulatory problems in his legs forced him to seek medical attention, he ran out of money and hope. Evicted from his apartment while in the hospital, he arrived home to discover all his possessions, including his guitar, had been sold by the landlord.

He lost his home, his friends, and his career, and he fell into depression.

Social workers who helped Darnell get off the streets had trouble lifting his spirits. His life had been in a downward spiral, and he had no interest in the future.

Then they realized how important it was to help Darnell get a guitar. "I had given up and lost the will, until I got the guitar," Darnell explains. "When people play an instrument, they feel in control. The world is on a string, and it's just the way you want it to be."

With guitar in hand, Darnell has a purpose and a passion. With guitar in hand, even with all the troubles he's endured, he has hope. "At the end of each tunnel, there's a light. I kind of see the light now. And you know something? I may not walk so fast, but I'm walking. So I'm on my way."

Research comparing students of similar ability finds that the distinguishing feature between those who maintain a strong work ethic in their studies and those who give up is a sense of control. Those who express a sense of control receive scores that are a full letter grade higher than those who do not. (Mendoza 1999)

52

Life Is Not a Zero-Sum Game

Deciding how to spend money without going into debt is a zero-sum process. If you want to spend more on housing, you will have to spend less on your car. Every additional expenditure has to be matched with an equal reduction in spending.

Some people view their lives in much the same way. If they want a career, they have to sacrifice family time. If they want a family life, they have to sacrifice their career.

But this equation is incomplete and misleading. Your time is not literally an accounting of minutes, like your budget is an accounting of dollars. Your time is a measure of commitment, concern, and efficiency, not just quantity.

You can do more when you use your time better. Take out a few frivolous time killers and work harder at using time well, and you can add to both sides of your life's equation.

"MY FATHER GAVE me a book of lawyer jokes; I've heard them all," says Michigan attorney Douglas Theodoroff. "Sometimes lawyers get a bad rap, but we probably deserve it."

Douglas is known as one of the good guys, a lawyer who takes time out from his thriving practice to donate it to clients who cannot afford to pay.

"I almost consider myself a legal social worker. I enjoy solving problems for people. I have something I can share. If I can help people less fortunate, I want to do it."

Douglas says that even though he has a heavy workload, it's never overwhelming because he imposes some order on it. "As you get older, it's easier to establish your priorities and not feel pressured to take on every paying client available," he explains.

Douglas also serves his clients' interests and his own time demands by trying to find solutions out of the courtroom. "Going to court is the most expensive and time-consuming outcome; it should be a last resort."

The quantity of hours spent working or thinking about work, or hours spent with our families, does not predict achievement or life satisfaction. Instead, the quality of those hours—how stressful or relaxing they are—is a much more potent factor in producing a satisfying family life and career. (Brown 1999)

53

You Don't Have to Get Straight A's Anymore

We all remember our first performance evaluation. Report cards. We carried them home and presented them to our parents, yearning for their approval.

From a very early age we were taught the significance of outcomes. Whether it was getting a dollar for every A, being given a smile or kind word, or avoiding being grounded, we discovered the report card mattered and we needed to be good at what we did.

We still carry this formative lesson of contingent approval with us. We still seek success to win approval, some of us from parents or spouses, others from colleagues and supervisors.

But just as having to get good grades to please your parents did not instill a love of reading, having to succeed to attain the approval of someone else will not make you enjoy the process.

To succeed, not just in the outcome but in the process, you need to invest the effort for yourself, not to win approval from others.

ANN ORTIZ BEGAN Ann's Turquoise with a vision, about fifteen hundred dollars, and plenty of patience. Her vision was to create a unique retail store that featured clothing, jewelry, and crafts that couldn't be found anywhere in the Topeka area, or anyplace else for that matter.

To do it right, Ann realized she had to take her time. "We've done this as a slow process, because if we tried to grow too fast, we wouldn't be able to maintain our purpose."

Ann's store is doing better than she could have imagined—and she someday might consider opening a second location when the time is right. She says opening a store taught her "that if you really enjoy and love something, it shows through your work. It's shown me what an individual can accomplish. What you do doesn't have to be the biggest, best business in the world to be your business, to fulfill your dream."

More than nine out of ten people felt, when they were children, some need to demonstrate competence to earn or deserve parental love. For most, this pattern remains in adulthood as they continue to use their career to seek approval from loved ones despite the anxiety and disappointment this pattern can produce. (Jones and Berglas 1999)

54

Whet Your Appetite for Success

Appetite is an instinctive human regulatory device. We do not have to do anything to create it; it is already there. We were born with some level of appetite necessary to keep us alive.

Motivation for achievement is also an instinctive human regulatory device. We do not have to do anything to create it; it is already there. We were born with some level of motivation necessary to keep us alive.

Because appetite and motivation are instinctive, they predate our knowledge of their existence. But that doesn't mean we are powerless to change them. We already know how to regulate appetite: drink two big glasses of water before a meal, and you will reduce your appetite for food.

In the same way, we can kill or whet our appetite for success. If you spend your time worrying and impatiently awaiting an easy life, you will reduce your motivation for success. If, on the other hand, you pursue activities you really care about, your motivation will increase.

Cultivate your instincts in the direction you want them to lead you, and your growing motivation will make the pursuit of success easier.

"I WAS the kind of student that really upset the teachers," says Herbert Brennan, "because they believed I could be a good student but I never tried very hard. All through high school, I was no more than mediocre—listlessly going through the motions of chemistry, algebra, history, English, and the rest."

Herbert says he barely made it into the local state college, "and when I got there, I loafed my way through the placement exams, barely scoring outside of the remedial range."

Sometime early in his freshman year, everything changed. "I remember the feeling to this day because it was so shocking. I was sitting down to read a book for my history class, and it hit me that I was happy about it. I was looking forward to opening the book and investing myself in it."

Herbert graduated with honors with a degree in history and then went on to graduate school, ultimately to become a professor. "I became a different student when I found a subject I loved, and I was unstoppable once I knew what it was."

Long-term studies of motivation find that people are capable of reducing or improving their level of motivation by as much as 58 percent during their careers. (Alderman 1999)

55

Remember the Difference Between You and Everybody Else

Turn on the evening news, and you'll see another day's catalog of terror and trauma. Read the business page, and you'll see which local company is downsizing. Our big-picture perspective can be shaped, or misshaped, by attention-grabbing events.

The news doesn't cover people who had a particularly good day and return home to their happy families. The news doesn't cover the continued existence of a healthy company.

Don't let the negative picture of the world cloud your perspective.

ANTHONY JOHNSON, a physics professor at the New Jersey Institute of Technology, works with lasers that travel in femtoseconds, a million times faster than nanoseconds.

Anthony is the son of a bus driver, from a family where every male drove a bus or a train for a living. Almost everyone he knew growing up struggled just to keep up with the bills and keep a roof over their heads.

But Anthony saw a path for himself in high school, then college, and finally graduate school. And now he is on the lookout for the next generation of physicists.

"Too many young people have written science off; that's a real tough battle we have. If we don't show students an example, they won't dream of careers in science or anything else. Too many give up because there's so much 'give up' around them."

Anthony explains he wouldn't have gotten where he is "without some great people who invested in me and helped me see what I could do." He adds, "I'm not just going to sit here without going to the next generation and showing them what we do here. Because what we do could shape the future."

People are seven times more likely to be optimistic about their personal future than they are about the future of their generation. (Arnett 2000)

56

Your Work and Home Lives Must Fit Together

E ven if 99.9 percent of the parts of your car are in perfect shape, a defective 0.1 percent that includes a flat tire or a dead battery means your car can't be used.

Much of your life can be healthy and satisfying, but if an important part of it is not working well, you will not feel fulfilled.

Successful living is not a matter of success in the workplace or success at home; it is the product of their combination.

EDWIN AND VICKIE Weatherspoon began as partners in life and then became partners in business.

The California couple had been married for three years when they decided Vickie should join her husband's business, which offers janitorial services for corporate clients.

Husband and wife working together—a dream come true? Hardly. "It was difficult at first," Vickie explained, since both had their ideas about how things should be done. "We're both power players. We'd step over boundaries and take it home."

They committed themselves over time to putting their two worlds in balance. "We learned how to keep our personal lives separate and how to stay friends at the end of the day. By the same token, if we're at home or on vacation or out with friends, we won't be talking business all the time."

Vickie and Edwin credit their business success to the foundation they had first in their relationship. "That helps us keep perspective on what's really most important."

People at the peak of their careers report that reaching their goals in work increases their commitment to their home life because they feel a great sense of security, which improves their time outside of work. (Persley 1998)

57

Nobody Wins Without a Loser

On the path to success, you will sometimes confront situations in which you must directly compete with someone and your victory will create bitterness. Even more frequently, your success will cause others to compare themselves to you and to react with jealousy at your ability.

Take comfort in the knowledge that it is not a personal attack on you but instead a sincere but unpleasant form of flattery.

"EVERY YEAR, I spend less time talking around the water cooler," says Sheila. "As you advance up the corporate ladder, a lot of people begin to think of you as the enemy instead of a friend who happens to have been promoted."

Sheila struggles with the implications of her rapid rise through the ranks of the financial services company where she works. "At the same time, you can't sit around wishing away success so that your co-workers will like you again."

The best advice on the matter came from her father, who toiled for forty-five years without achieving the advancements his daughter had in less than ten. He said to Sheila, "Treat everyone with respect, and don't treat anyone, above or below you, based on their station. Eventually, that respect will come back to you."

Six in ten top managers report that they have lost friendships among co-workers who were not promoted as fast as they were. (Austin 2000)

58

Tell Clean Jokes

Humor captures people's attention and sets them at ease. However, there is a major difference between positive humor and negative humor. Negative humor involves attacks on people or their ideas or focuses on areas of behavior that would not be discussed at the dinner table. Positive humor involves silliness, and if there is any target of the humor at all, it is the joke teller.

In the workplace, use positive humor freely and negative humor not at all.

LOUIS SIEGFRIED RUNS a multimillion-dollar mail order business selling computers. While he takes his business seriously, he also takes having a positive attitude seriously. "I think if you have fun, then you do well. We can't tolerate people who aren't enthusiastic."

Louis seeks employees who want to work, and he strives for a workplace where they'll want to work. "Whether it's meetings, memos, or policies, most business seems to operate on the premise that if you can possibly make something boring, make it extra boring. We operate under the rule that the best way to get people to do their job well is to get them to want to do their job, and the best way to do that is to make sure there's a little fun in what we do."

When negative humor is used in the workplace, it tends to spread throughout the organization; 41 percent see it as a source of division in their office. Widespread positive humor, on the other hand, increases job satisfaction by 5 percent. (Decker and Rotondo 1999)

59

Don't Want Everything

We think of many aspects of life as a race—who gets the promotion, who gets the biggest salary, who has the nicest car. It's a race between us and everyone around us for these things.

Yet we don't all need to have these things to succeed. What we need is what we need. Because someone else wants to be at the top or have the most or work the longest hours does not mean that you need those same things.

Success in life is not a matter of getting everything. That's impossible and wouldn't be much of a joy even if it were possible. Success is a matter of getting what you need.

Think of success as filling a box. You'll be finished sooner not just by working harder to fill it but also by choosing a smaller box.

BECKY CONSIDERS herself normal in most respects. She has a career, a husband, two children, and almost no time.

"Do you ever feel like you woke up in an episode of *Twilight Zone?* My story is the person who constantly has more things to do and less time in which to do it. It's like every day I have to make more runs to the store than the day before, and I have to do it in half the time."

Becky concluded that the key to living life at her own pace, instead of in a rushed hurry, was "to realize what is really important. I spent so much time doing things because I thought I was supposed to instead of because they were really necessary."

To get out of her Twilight Zone, Becky stopped going after everything. "If you run out of time trying to do absolutely everything, then sometimes you wind up finishing the stupid stuff and missing out on what really matters."

What success means is not universal. Studies of people who have attained nearly identical achievements in the workplace, for example, find great variation in their level of satisfaction, with some considering themselves tremendously successful and others considering themselves average or even failures. (Maasen and Landsheer 2000)

60

Look for Value

W hen we first meet people, our natural inclination is to size them up—to create an immediate impression of their abilities and liabilities.

Unfortunately, we often hold on to these vague and hasty conclusions and never revise them. This means we can easily overlook the talents of people we have written off based on superficial information.

Many people know to search for the overlooked value when they are buying something, but there is also great potential for overlooked value in the people around you.

YEARS WENT BY, and Jane wondered if anybody was ever going to ask her to do anything more challenging than count. Her job was to monitor the assembly lines at a cosmetics manufacturer. Each hour she took note of the production level of each line and sent the information to the floor manager.

Jane counted output, matched it with a count of materials used, and then did it all over again. Nobody asked her why the lines were slow or fast. That wasn't her job. Just count.

Over the course of five years, Jane took note of a hundred factors that influenced the pace of the lines, factors she knew nobody else was paying attention to. For one, if the volume on the radio system was too low, the workers spoke to each other more often, slowing down their pace.

The general manager casually asked her one time how things were going, expecting a generic response. He nearly fell over when Jane said production was down 2 percent and offered a list of the three most likely explanations.

Jane finally became visible to management, and she was promoted to a job where she could put to use many of the observations she'd made over the years.

· Researchers find that the tendency to quickly assess abilities in other people is thought by many to be a highly valuable skill. In truth, this habit actually reduces productivity and increases turnover. One of the key characteristics of successful business leaders, according to 61 percent of them, is a willingness to engage in revitalization of employees, actively trying to see what workers are capable of and then helping them achieve that. (Boyer 1999)

61

Get Your Motivation Where You Can Find It

People who care do a better job in everything they do.

Why do people care? What inspires them? The answer is almost anything you can imagine.

Some people are driven internally by their own competitive juices. Some are driven externally by their thirst for approval and appreciation. Some are driven by a desire to succeed for their families, while others are driven to succeed to show up their families.

Use what you really care about to make yourself passionate about how things turn out.

"I'D RATHER BECOME a furniture mover" is how seventy-year-old Lorna responded when her doctor told her she needed to exercise regularly. She said exercise would bore her out of her mind.

Lorna and her doctors realized that exercising was so unappealing to Lorna that she was unlikely to follow through with it on her own. So her doctors helped place her in a women's exercise group that met three times a week at the University of Wisconsin.

While she was no great fan of the exercise regimen, it was the fifty other women in the group who first changed Lorna's attitude. "The wonderful women kept me coming back. It's one of the neatest groups of women I've ever met in my life. They have depth to them."

Over time, the rewards of the exercise brought their own joy to Lorna's life. "When I first started with this group I had back trouble and had laser surgery on my knee and a lot of pains and stiffness. But I'm back now. I can twirl and jitterbug every bit as good as I did when I was a kid. So that's amazing."

When tested in national surveys against such seemingly crucial factors as intelligence, ability, and salary, level of motivation proves to be a more significant component in predicting career success. While level of motivation is highly correlated with success, importantly, the source of motivation varies greatly among individuals and is unrelated to success. (Bashaw and Grant 1994)

62

Be an Expert

Members of Congress vote on thousands of issues every year. The issues are prominent and obscure, domestic and foreign, things everybody thinks about all the time and things almost no one in the world ever thinks about.

How do they do it? How can they possibly cope with all those issues at the same time?

They rely on a system of expertise. Members specialize in particular areas and share their expertise when "their" issue comes up for a vote.

The advantage of being the expert, of course, is that others listen to your thoughts and perspective because they have less knowledge and information. The expert then relies on others when a new subject comes up.

Choose a particular area that is crucial to what you do, and learn everything you can about it. There is no better way to ensure that you will be invaluable and that your suggestions will be respected and followed.

FRED WILBER has sold quirky and hard-to-find music out of his store in Montpelier, Vermont, for twenty-seven years. He worried that the Internet, and specifically the giant Web retailers who seemed to be able to sell everything, might spell the end of his business.

So he decided to go on-line himself. Fred has neither the resources nor the inclination to do battle with the Web superstores, so he designed his Web site as an on-line version of his physical store. It features items that reflect his peculiar tastes and unmatched knowledge of movie soundtracks.

Spotlighting his own expertise is bringing in business. "You can go anywhere to buy the latest hit CD, but who is going to tell you about a great CD you've never heard of? Let alone track down a copy of an out-of-print movie soundtrack of *Gordy! The Little Pig that Hit it Big!* I can do those kinds of things, and no one else can."

By "focusing on our own niche, what we know best," Fred has watched his combined in-store and on-line sales grow by over 10 percent a year and his customer base by 20 percent.

Sixty-eight percent of people who consider themselves successful say that there is at least one area of their job in which they are an expert. (Austin 2000)

63

Failure Is Not Trying

The fear of failure is powerful. Nobody wants to reveal to others, or to themselves, that they were not capable of doing something they tried to do.

This fear can be used as a source of motivation to keep you working hard toward your goals. Yet this same fear offers a convenient escape clause. You can never fail if you don't bother to try.

Not trying is, of course, the ultimate failure, for it means you can never make progress toward your goals.

JEFF HOWARD is a school psychologist who studies how we teach youngsters and how they learn. He says most school systems informally break their student body into three groups: the very smart, the kind-of smart, and the kind-of dumb. By the time they reach the sixth grade, those consigned to the kind-of-dumb group are already well versed in the low expectations educators have for them.

"We put up barriers to these children in middle school, barriers we don't expect them to climb over, barriers that they shouldn't have to climb over." For example, schools in Japan require every high school student to take calculus, while schools in the United States reserve calculus for the very smart. Howard argues that every student has the capacity to learn more—that studies of the learning capacity of your average four-year-old are more optimistic than the treatment received by the kind-of-dumb middle schooler.

The real danger in these categories is the big lesson they teach. For the top group, anything is possible, so they should never stop trying. For the bottom group, nothing is possible, so they shouldn't bother trying. Indeed, these students mock their classmates who care or try to succeed.

Howard's experimental solution involves putting students of all levels together and placing clear expectations and rewards in front of all of them. Early results show that all students, from all three levels, improved their test scores when expectations were increased.

When asked to describe significant regrets in their lives, more than eight out of ten people focused on actions they did not take rather than actions they did. In other words, they focused on things they failed to do rather than things they failed at doing. (Ricaurte 1999)

64

You Are Not in This Alone

The American dream. The American work ethic. The American pioneer spirit.

If you listen to the slogans, you can't help but think it's everyone for themselves and that every person's success or failure is completely their own.

Thinking and feeling this way feeds a certain sense of desperation. Everyone is tempted to think, "The outcome is riding on me. Everything that happens, or doesn't happen, is because of me."

Realistically, though, no one is completely on their own. Every step of the way, we have met people who protected us and taught us. And for all the power of the American individualistic spirit, no one, not even pioneers, has succeeded alone.

DECADES AGO, Milwaukee's King Drive was a thriving retail center. Then hard times fell on the surrounding neighborhood and the businesses lining King Drive.

Today, the street is making a comeback, spurred by entrepreneurs who are working together to help one another and the community. Business owners have formed an association and have worked to have sites on the street declared historic buildings.

They also offer training and loans to new King Drive business owners because, as Lennie Mosely, who moved her already-established business to King Drive, explains, "We want to have more of a stake in the community. You talk about having a dream. Well, our dreams are happening here.

"We make it clear to everybody who gives this place a try: 'You are not in this by yourself, we're in this together.'"

Said one urban planning researcher of their efforts, "From what I've seen around the country, King Drive stands out as one of the best examples of inner-city redevelopment."

People who acknowledge the interdependent nature of life, the importance of human connections and our collective existence, were twice as likely to consider themselves successful as those who held completely individualistic views. (Carpenter 2000)

65

Your Goals Are a Living Thing

Goals have to evolve with you. They should be neither absurdly out of reach nor easily within reach. In either case, your motivation will be stalled by the uselessness of your goals.

Keep your goals far enough away that you need to keep trying but close enough that you can someday reach them.

IN 1978 KUMIKO Watanuki had her career goal set on eventually running the Iranian division of AT&T. Then revolution engulfed the country. She found herself forced out of the country and having to start over in the New York office, without any map for the future.

She set out to create a new career plan and capitalized on the advantages of being back in the United States. "I had the chance now to pursue a master's degree that the company would pay for, and I had access to company personnel I never could have met working half a world away."

Advancement to the upper echelon of the company did not seem likely, however, and Kumiko realized her international experience could be put to better use. Today, she runs a company that advises on international trade matters.

"I worked with a five-year plan of what I needed to do and what I wanted to accomplish. I've followed it, even though I had to take some detours, and I'm right where I want to be. I made my career plan an integral part of my life."

Research on recent college graduates finds that 70 percent react to negative early experiences in the workplace by becoming defensive about their abilities. Because they shun feedback in the aftermath of a setback at work, they have trouble adapting their outlook and habits to help them succeed. (Trope and Pomerantz 1998)

66

Avoid Roller-Coaster Emotions

Everybody likes some excitement in their world. But the heights of feeling good are usually followed by the depths of feeling bad.

A successful life is not to be found in one exciting day but in a steady, productive, fulfilling career.

TONY AND CARLA made it through the lean years. He was still in school. She worked hard to pay for their expenses and then came home and worked hard to cook meals and keep their home in order and generally makes things as nice as she could for Tony.

"Back then," Carla remembers, "it was an uphill struggle, but it was our uphill struggle. And we just kept on going, with each other."

And now, degree in hand, Tony has reached new heights. Financial struggles are gone. In fact, almost everything of their early married life is gone. Instead of expressing satisfaction, he rants against the fact that Carla hasn't become a new person to match the new person he is.

Carla worries about what it means. "I don't want everything to change. I don't want to be a new person. I don't want to live every day anxious about whether I'm good enough or I'm going to do something that disappoints him again."

Tony tells her she ignored the part about marriage being for better not worse, and she's ruining the better.

Carla, for her part, longs for the time "when our lives were steady. It was hard, but it was steady."

Long-term studies of corporate leaders find that seven in ten of those who survive longest in their jobs downplay both the best and worst outcomes they experience and keep their feelings relatively steady. They have what psychologists call a "focus on an acceptable average," not on the extraordinary, which is useful because almost every day turns out to be more average than extraordinary. (Ingram 1998)

67

Care

Whether at home or at work, people who find their lives fulfilling care about those around them.

They invest themselves in those around them, actively concerning themselves with their lives, concerns, interests, and well-being.

WHEN HIS TEXTILE mill burned down in December of 1995, Malden Mills owner Aaron Feuerstein suffered a terrible blow. He'd invested heavily, both with his money and his life, in keeping his business thriving in the face of foreign competition, which paid its workers inhuman wages and could therefore undercut his prices.

When the architects, contractors, and accountants tallied up the costs of rebuilding, Aaron worried about whether the business could go on. But the more he thought about the business, the more he thought about the more than two thousand people who worked for him—people who came in every morning and worked hard all day, turning out a quality product that had brought in profits even when everybody else said it couldn't be done.

Aaron made a decision then that not only would he rebuild his mill, he would also keep paying his employees while the mill was closed during the months of construction work ahead. Tears of sorrow at what happened to the plant, and what would happen to them, turned to tears of joy on his workers' faces.

Today, the plant is up and running, and Malden Mills workers are, according to Aaron, "about the most loyal and hardworking people you could ever meet."

Eight in ten CEOs report that a healthy family life is crucial to a productive business life and that the same key skill—"interpersonal engagement," the capacity to express concern and interest in those around them—is crucial to both home and work. (Henderson 1999)

You Can't Be Persistent
Without Perspective

M ost of the things you really want are not going to come to you overnight, this week, or next month. Most of what is truly important to you will take years, sometimes a lot longer.

How can you go on, knowing that you have so much further to go?

Persistent people arm themselves with the knowledge that what they want can be done. They focus not on the distance they must go to get what they want, but on the belief that what they want is possible, that they can do it. Persistent people also understand that as important as it is to understand the task in front of them, it is even more important to understand themselves and the perspective they have on the future.

SOMETIMES HE has trouble convincing even his wife, but investment adviser John Conover tells everyone that the stock market is a great long-term investment.

"There is no better long-term investment. Disciplined, long-term investing in a diversified group of stocks is not sexy or thrilling or likely to make you rich overnight. But then again, there isn't anything that's going to make you rich overnight."

He explains, "Good companies with good products will make money, and in the long run their stock will appreciate. There will be dips, because of weak years for the company or the economy overall, but patience will guarantee that you hold the stock when the good years come. And the good years will outnumber the bad."

Trying for immediate returns from stocks, to John is "a fool's game. It's hazardous to your financial health and something I recommend only if you want to lose all your investments rather than make money."

Comparing people who tend to give up easily with people who tend to carry on, even through difficult challenges, researchers find that persistent people spend twice as much time thinking, not about what has to be done, but about what they have already accomplished, the fact that the task is doable, and that they are capable of it. (Sparrow 1998)

69

Changing Jobs Doesn't Change You

Transitions intimidate us because everything seems so different. But even though our surroundings change, we don't change.

We need some stability in our lives to be able to function. When you undertake new things, rely on the stability of who you are to provide you comfort and confidence.

AMY IS A career counselor who sees people changing jobs every day. She also sees people fall into transition anxiety all the time: "It's like sending a five-year-old off to the first day of kindergarten. What's it going to be like? What will happen to me? The fears some people have would be funny if they weren't so real."

Amy focuses her clients' attention on the one thing that doesn't change with a career move: themselves. "Some people lose all sense of proportion and really think everything in their world will change. Some look at that change as positive, as if all their old bad habits will fall away. I compare changing jobs to changing relationships. You wouldn't just change relationships to solve your infidelity problem because you would just bring the problem with you. And you can't just change jobs to make yourself into a new person. You'll be the same wherever you work, and work will be what you make of it wherever you go."

Nearly everyone feels some anxiety when starting a new job. However, people who focus their attention on their own identity rather than their uncertain surroundings feel less stress and report becoming comfortable in their new position in half as much time. (Elovainio and Mivimaeki 2001)

70

It Might Get Worse
Before It Gets Better

The things you most want aren't easy to get; otherwise you would already have them. We are faced with the daunting fact that in an effort to pursue our goals, to ultimately make our lives better, we must first endure and sacrifice.

You could minimize your efforts now, which would offer momentary comfort but leave you ill suited to achieve in the future, or you could maximize your effort now and create an ideal future.

"I BOUGHT a nightclub without really understanding what I was getting into," says Dean Maples. "My partners were convinced it should be renovated before we opened, and suddenly my costs had tripled.

"Then we opened, and for a year the crowds were so small I could have fit them in my living room," he says with some exaggeration.

His experts told him it was time for a new name, a new theme, and new management. But that would mean shutting the place down and spending even more money. "We'd already endured and sacrificed, and there was nothing to be gained by giving up now."

Today, the Pacifica club opens to massive crowds and generates big profits. "You can't create something like this overnight," Dean says with relief and pride.

Among managers in upper-level positions, 84 percent report having had to deal with a "period of discomfort" in their lives. Some took career risks, worked long hours, or acquired new skills, but they saw the sacrifice as necessary to pursue employment, promotion, and success. (Atkinson 1999)

71

If You Don't Believe, No One Else Will

Sometimes we look to others to convince us of what we want to believe. "I can do it, can't I?" we ask.

Ironically, others base their true judgments, not just on what they think we can do, but on what they think we think we can do. In other words, the people around you will most likely mirror your feelings—showing you fear when you show fear and confidence when you demonstrate confidence.

You can't rely on others to convince you because they will rely on you to convince them.

PAUL GONZALES grew up in a poor Los Angeles neighborhood. He remembers the occasional career day when successful people would visit his school and tell the students a little about what they did. Paul says those visits did little for him because he could never see himself in their place.

As he grew up, he witnessed a barrage of violence, culminating in the murder of a cousin. Paul decided that he had to make a change, "That day, I made a promise to myself. I would never make sorrow for others. I would make joy for what I accomplished."

As a fourteen-year-old, Paul turned away from the neighborhood gangs that were all around him and began training with the local police athletic league. "I knew I had to do something for myself," Paul explained about a regime that began with 5:00 AM workouts. Ultimately he chose boxing as his sport and set his sights on the Olympics.

In 1984 Paul made the U.S. Olympic boxing team and went on to win a gold medal. He's now a guest at career days in Los Angeles, and he tells students the most important thing they need to learn is: "You can do anything you want, but you have to believe in yourself first."

People were five times more likely to be optimistic about another person's goals if they thought the person was optimistic themselves. Less significant factors included the person's personal experiences and the overall likelihood of the outcome. (Werneck De Almeida 1999)

72

You'll Work Harder if You Feel Wanted

It might sound small, but it's true. We work harder and better when we feel appreciated.

Money, prestige, and all the other aspects of work we benefit from will be compromised if we do not think that those we work for care about us.

WAINWRIGHT INDUSTRIES of Missouri says its average employee generates fifty-five ideas per year to improve the company's production of automotive and aerospace parts.

Wainwright's chairperson, Don Wainwright, credits his company's attitude toward employees for fostering creativity. "In most organizations, the managers operate like parents who make the rules and then administer punishments and rewards. The nonmanagers play a corollary role of children who have to be good and do what Mom and Dad say, or else."

At Wainwright, he says, they adopted a People First Policy. The new policy "avoids this parent trap and encourages every employee to speak up when they have a better idea instead of either making the suggestion to a superior, who might then steal credit as the idea works its way up the line, or, ultimately, not saying anything at all."

The policy has been a huge success, and Don Wainwright credits it for a 35 percent drop in production costs and a 91 percent drop in customer rejection rates. It also helped bring home the coveted Malcolm Baldridge National Quality Award.

Lower-management workers who felt like they were appreciated by superiors were 52 percent less likely to look for a different job. (Jones 2000)

73

Don't Talk to Yourself

Answers that seem obvious to us appear that way because of our perspective—everything we know about the subject and everything we have experienced. When we communicate our ideas, though, we need to consider not just what makes sense to us but what would make sense if we looked at the situation with a completely different background.

A presentation is the best expression of your ideas, not to an audience consisting of you, but to an audience that has never seen the world through your eyes.

RETTEW ASSOCIATES, an engineering firm in New York and Pennsylvania, surveys and plans parks, roadways, and developments.

In little more than a decade it has grown from a four-person operation to a company generating ten million dollars a year out of five separate divisions.

Founder George Rettew credits much of its success to bringing together different services under one roof. "If we can be the only firm a client has to deal with on a project, it makes life a little easier on them."

Combining services is not without difficulty, though, since, as George notes, "geologists and engineers speak a different language and think differently." To overcome those problems, both for the sake of his clients and to keep his different divisions functioning well, George puts great emphasis on communication. "We need to step back and listen to each other because there is a lot we can teach each other if we do this right."

A study of consultants showed that 82 percent found studying an organization's founding and long-term culture critical to improving their ability to successfully communicate innovations. (Smith 2000)

74

Seek Coherence and Congruence

Individual decisions might seem ideal, but placed in the context of a larger series of plans, those same decisions might not make any sense at all. Your goals, your plans, your daily activities and habits can't be evaluated in isolation from one another.

Your purpose is to make, not a series of independent decisions that by themselves make sense, but a series of decisions that together make sense for your life.

WHEN ISABEL and Michael were about to become parents, they agreed on the need for one of them to stay home with the baby. Without really discussing the situation, both assumed Isabel would resign from her job as a nurse. They thought it was the natural thing to do; when a parent needs to stay home, it's the mother's responsibility.

Isabel went on maternity leave and gave birth to a bouncing baby girl. While still on maternity leave, however, Isabel began to rethink her decision. Her income was higher than her husband's. Her medical benefits were better. What sense did it make for her to leave her job when she had the better job?

They discussed it, and although Michael was surprised at the idea, he could not argue with the financial advantages.

It took some getting used to for Michael, not earning an income and being dependent on Isabel's salary. But the decision made sense for the family, as Michael could see. "Isabel's salary is the family's money, and our daughter is the best career anyone could ask for."

Fewer than two in ten people use a decision-making strategy that addresses how their decisions fit into all phases of their life, including those that appear unrelated. Most people make decisions by examining only factors that seem directly related. (Ichniowski, Levine, Olsen, and Strauss 2000)

75

If You Doubt, You're Out

Confidence is like a helpful virus spreading throughout your body. If you have it, it will infect everything you do in a positive way. If you don't, it will undermine everything you do.

People who lack confidence not only fear doing things they are not good at, they actually start to fear performing tasks in which they excel because they question whether they're all that good at anything.

Confidence spreads with successes, and lack of confidence multiplies with failures. If your confidence falters, turn to what you do best, and then take on more challenging tasks.

MARGARET HAS BEEN an attorney for over thirty years. She handles a variety of civil cases and has earned a reputation as a fierce litigator.

It wasn't always that way for Margaret, though. "In the beginning, I faced all the barriers that were in place against women and all the slights that occurred. Judges would lecture you about appropriate hairstyles for the courtroom, what you should wear. When a judge entered the room, he would say, 'Good morning, gentlemen,' as if I wasn't even there. Opposing counsel would look over at you like you were a little girl."

It was upsetting and intimidating. But getting rattled by the slights wasn't doing her any good, and it wasn't doing her clients any good. "I tried to look for some way out of the situation, and I realized that these attitudes could be used to my advantage. Yes, I was being treated with condescension, but that means they were underestimating me. I began to approach everything with a different perspective—and their minor slights were actually making me more confident."

While the insults have thankfully waned over the years, Margaret's confidence has remained an important part of her legal skills.

People who feel less talented than those around them actually believe they will be outperformed in any task they might be asked to complete, ranging from knowledge tests to creativity exercises and even games. (Mayo and Christenfeld 1999)

76

Always Think About What's Next

Imagine the average workplace of 1900—a place without the Internet, without computers of any kind, without calculators, without even electricity in many places.

When people look back on 2001, what tools will they marvel that we functioned without? What devices will become commonplace that nobody has yet even imagined?

Those who are more capable of dealing with the future and the changes it holds are those who do not fear change and who practice flexibility. Your job will not be the same in twenty years no matter what it is like today. But that doesn't mean you won't excel in the future. It just means you need to embrace innovation because those who fail to do so will not stay on top.

BARRY AND JUDY Wirth own ProPet, an independent pet store in central Pennsylvania. The Wirths watched as pet superstores moved into surrounding towns. These chains had massive stores, incredible selection, and the buying power to lower prices on dog food, the biggest-selling item in the pet store business.

While Barry and Judy knew what it took to succeed with a small business that filled a unique niche, they had no idea how to stare down the challenge of thriving in the face of big and powerful competition.

"I looked at every aspect of what we did—and looked for things we could do better," Barry explains. Although they had long appreciated the freedom of being completely independent, the Wirths decided the future lay with a pet supply cooperative that allowed small stores to operate with the collective buying power of hundreds of others.

Barry says the continued success of the store is dependent on one thing: "We need to keep up with the future direction of this business. If you don't change to keep up, you're going to be blindsided."

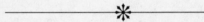

Research on employees who experienced layoffs that had nothing to do with their job performance found that flexibility, a willingness to try new tasks and learn new skills, was the single best predictor of how long people stayed unemployed. (Ingram 1998)

77

Value Practical Knowledge

Every year millions of young people finish school full of confidence and self-importance and arrive in the workplace only to find out how much they don't know.

Don't overlook the great importance of the practical knowledge you have and the importance of the practical knowledge you can gain by learning every aspect about the things you do.

PATTY GRIFFIN SPENT years on the coffeehouse circuit, looking for any chance to play her music for an audience. The New England native was thrilled when she finally got her big break, a contract with A&M Records.

She found a veteran producer and plunged headfirst into the studio to record. After an exhausting two months of studio work, she had an album to play for the record company.

They immediately rejected it.

Patty realized that it wasn't a rejection of her so much as a rejection of the process that she had followed, one where her input was ignored. "My voice got lost in the production. It became the producer's record, not mine. It was very far from the direction I wanted to go."

She wondered what would happen if she sent the record company copies of her songs recorded in practice sessions, songs recorded without a producer or a professional band. "I knew better what I could do—how to bring my voice, figuratively and literally, into a record."

Despite the fact that some of the songs were performed while Patty was sitting at a kitchen table, the record company loved them as she had originally created them.

With her songs as she wanted them intact on the album, Patty took a lesson about making her music and not "worrying about what everybody else would do."

Knowledge gained through workplace experience was six times more important than grades earned in school in predicting job performance of new employees. (Sternberg, Forsythe, Hedlund, Horvath, Wagner, Williams, Snook, and Grigorenko 2000)

78

See the Risk in Doing Nothing

Watch a football game, and you'll hear the announcers talking about the risks coaches face, especially the risks associated with trying to score. Announcers caution against throwing the ball too much or taking a chance by going for a big play. What they fail to talk about is the risk of not trying these things.

Yes, coaches risk turning the ball over, and possibly losing the game, by creatively trying to score. However, there is a very real risk that in trying to avoid these outcomes, coaches will be so conservative that they will lose the game because they didn't take any risks and couldn't accomplish anything.

Managing your career is much like that. You can easily see the risk associated with going for the big score (such as applying for a new job or accepting new responsibilities). But there is a very real risk in not doing these things. If ultimately you want more, whether it is responsibility, recognition, reward, or just a different challenge, failing to take a risk is the biggest risk of all because you will shut off possible opportunities.

WILLIAM WENT to work each day at the General Mills plant. The work was hard and dirty, but it was steady and William was not one to complain. Each night he came home, ate dinner, and then picked up his paintbrush.

William painted street scenes that depicted harsh realities of city life. He painted every night for years. His works were displayed only in his closets and spare bedroom. He showed them to no one. In fact, he didn't like talking about his hobby at all if he could avoid it.

One of his friends practically begged William to enter one of his paintings in a local amateur art show. William refused. And refused again the next year. Finally, the third year, he gave in, and William found himself the winner of the grand prize.

Slowly, William overcame his reluctance and allowed some of his paintings to be shown in the public library in a feature of local artwork. A dealer found the work and had to do a lot of talking but finally convinced William to let her see more. A small show and the biggest check William had ever seen soon followed.

People who are satisfied with their careers are 48 percent more comfortable accepting some risk in their job future than people who feel unfulfilled in their work. Accepting risk not only makes them feel more comfortable pursuing future opportunities, it also allows them to feel that their current position is a choice rather than a sentence. (Ingram 1998)

79

Face Conflict Head-On

No matter what your career dream, it will at some point cause conflict in your home life. It is easier to pretend these conflicts do not exist or to dodge the matter whenever possible. But ignoring conflict doesn't make it go away; it just feeds the conflict and makes it worse.

Discuss conflicts between your work life and your home life because that is the only way you can make the situation better.

THE COALITION for Marriage, Family, and Couples Education teaches people that the surest path to resentment, strain, and relationship disaster is the complete absence of disagreements. Having no disagreements means you aren't saying what you think and feel and that emotions will simmer within you until they reach a boil.

One of the coalition's main lessons is that in any relationship there are "ten irreconcilable differences." According to Dianne Sollee, the director of the coalition, "The problem for most people is that they don't recognize that differences are inevitable and should be talked about, and they instead seek refuge from another relationship. Of course, their new relationship will have ten new irreconcilable differences, and the pattern will just be repeated."

Healthy relationships are successful, not because people have fewer disagreements, but because they apply problem-solving skills to arguments. Dianne says, "Instead of an emphasis on who is right and who is wrong, the underlying emphasis in healthy relationships is on what can be done to improve the situation for everyone involved."

Two-career couples were 56 percent more likely to express satisfaction with their marriage when they did not avoid dealing with conflicts and disagreements brought on by their work schedules. (Howell 1999)

80

Money Isn't Everything

Everybody wants a higher salary. People who have everything they need, even everything they want, still want a higher salary.

A paycheck has to be understood for what it truly represents. It is not just buying power or life security. To us it symbolizes the value placed in our efforts and abilities, the confidence others have in us.

In your quest for a bigger paycheck, remember what it means to you, and realize that respect for you can be demonstrated even without great financial rewards.

"HOW MUCH is an afternoon watching my son in the playground worth? For how many dollars would I sell you that day?" Beth asks herself these questions as she ponders whether or not to go back to work full-time.

"If I don't go back to work, there'll be no bigger house, no new car, but would I rather have those things than this chance to be a mother?" Beth hears these concerns all the time when she talks with other stay-at-home parents.

Although she has moments of doubt, in the end she says, "Money cannot be the measure of whether I've made the right decisions. If it were, I should work seven days a week, never have children, heck, never get married. There are more important things in life, and I shouldn't just say that but live like I believe it."

In national surveys comparing income with lifestyles and satisfaction (among people who have what's necessary to live on), salary increases have no effect on life satisfaction and little influence on work habits. (Eisenberger, Rhoades, and Cameron 1999)

81

Be Realistic About Yourself

Open up a motivational book, listen to a tape, attend a lecture, and you will hear all about the wonderful powers you possess and the amazing feats you are capable of. It is true that you must believe in yourself to succeed. To that extent, such a message is useful to you.

But an exaggerated sense of your abilities is no more valuable to you in the long run than a stunted sense of your abilities.

You do not, you should not, try to convince yourself you are Superman or Superwoman. You do yourself a disservice by trying to claim too many strengths because such an effort will ultimately undermine your confidence in the areas in which you do excel. Failure will be your kryptonite, and all your self-confidence powers will fade.

The best self-confidence is based on a realistic assessment of all your abilities, and it highlights the path to all your dreams.

BRUCE VOLUNTEERS as a youth soccer coach on the weekends in Tampa, Florida. He enjoys coaching children, teaching them techniques of the game, fitness, and teamwork.

But what really amazes him is what happens on the sidelines. "These parents think they are Vince Lombardi, 'Winning isn't everything, it's the only thing.' I'm focused on teaching the game, and hopefully sportsmanship, and the parents are running around like this is some cutthroat competition."

Bruce laments, "They scream at the refs. They scream at each other. They scream at the children. They make the kids feel like they are absolute failures anytime anything goes wrong in the game.

"It is really a devastating thing to watch—the joy of a child transformed into dejection because a parent comes to the game with the idea that their kid should be Pele instead of a seven-year-old having fun and getting some healthy exercise."

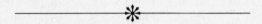

Confidence, in combination with a realistic self-appraisal, produces a 30 percent increase in life satisfaction. (Sedlacek 1999)

82

Find Your Own Path

Watch cars come off the assembly line, and you will see the same functions and capabilities in model after model. That's what they're designed for, that's how they're made. We buy them with the expectation that each will do the same thing, and the individual differences between cars are insignificant or nonexistent.

People, however, are not products off an assembly line. Even when we emerge from the same time and place, with the same training and upbringing, our differences are present from the start and will be present forever.

Before you try to live up to someone else's expectations, or reproduce someone else's success, ask yourself whether that is what you were really made for.

EDWARD BURKHARDT always wanted to work on the railroad. His first job as a teenager was working on the tracks doing maintenance. Later he was a brakeman, clerk, and machinist's helper. After finishing college, he joined the front office of the Wabash Railroad. His college classmates told him he was nuts—people don't get engineering degrees to work for a railroad, and the industry as a whole is dying.

After twenty years in the business, Edward put together a group to buy a regional railroad. The group bought the Wisconsin Central lines and began selling stock in the railroad in 1991. Even with many other railroad companies floundering, Wisconsin Central continued to produce a profit and saw its stock grow fifteenfold over the course of the decade. Despite the old-world imagery of the railroad industry, one of the biggest investors in Wisconsin Central is Microsoft founder Bill Gates.

For Edward, success in the railroads has been a wonderful ride. "Never be afraid to pursue your dreams. What else is there to pursue?"

Of people who feel they have failed to achieve success in their lives, 64 percent point to a specific standard set by others that they were unable to live up to. (Arnold 1995)

83

Own What You Do

It doesn't matter if you run a company or sort letters in the mail room; succeeding in what you do starts with taking ownership of the task.

You do it, therefore you do it well.

It doesn't matter what other people are doing or what senseless roadblocks are placed in your way by dumb policies or ill-chosen leaders. What you do represents your ability, commitment, and, ultimately, your potential to do something more.

TOM WILLIAMS began working for Apple Computer at the tender age of fourteen. While his relationship with the company eventually soured and he was forced out before the age of twenty, he refused to look past himself as the cause.

"I can't stand people who play the victim. None of this was anybody's choice but mine. No matter how impressionable or naive I have been, it has always been my decision."

At twenty-one, Tom works for a venture capital firm, evaluating the feasibility of new projects. He enjoys the great personal responsibility of the position; his recommendations could gain or lose millions for the company. "It's the decisions I make, good or bad, that give me the life I lead, not the economy, not a company, not anything else."

Satisfaction with work improved by 34 percent when employees felt they were individually responsible for their work output. (McCaw 1999)

84

Be Honest for Your Future

Few things are easier to lie about than the future. And few people are easier to lie to than ourselves.

It is therefore not surprising that people spend lifetimes lying to themselves about where they're going and why. It's easier to put off doing something difficult, and it's comforting to tell ourselves that we'll get around to it later.

But lying to ourselves about our goals is like paying off a loan by taking out an even bigger loan. It makes today easier, but it makes tomorrow much more difficult.

GREG INVESTED his life savings in the start-up costs of a handmade soap business in Oregon. There was only one problem. His handmade bars of soap turned to green mush when wet.

He'd already rented a booth in the mall and at an open market. He'd already had the labels printed. But his secret recipe for handmade soap was nothing short of a disaster.

Desperate and out of time, Greg bought soap from a wholesaler and slapped his label on it.

Greg told his customers it was handmade Oregon soap, though it was neither handmade nor from Oregon. He knew he was violating the terms of the lease for his market booth, which required him to sell only his own handmade merchandise, nothing else.

Although it would have been hard for him to be caught in the act, ultimately the fraud ate him up inside. He shut down the operation and faced, among other consequences, a ban on signing future leases at the market. Still, Greg's happy to be out of the deception. "If you have to lie about a fundamental aspect of your life, that builds an enormous complex in you and makes it seem like what you're doing is not even real."

People who consider their careers to have been successful are 81 percent less likely to have exaggerated their career plans when they were younger. (Ingram 1998)

85

You Need to Know
What You Are Looking For

What's the right direction for you? What career would suit your needs and abilities and help you realize your goals?

What most people focus on when they ask these questions is finding out about careers, getting more information about what's out there. But before you can make sense of what's out there, you need to understand yourself.

The details of a job are trivial compared to the importance of knowing who you are, what you can do, and what you want to do.

CINDY DEPPE owns one of the last drive-in movie theaters in Pennsylvania. Cindy faces the same pressures that have driven almost everyone else out of the drive-in business. The land is too expensive to use for movies. People don't want to sit in their cars when they can sit in air-conditioned theaters with reclining seats.

Yet Cindy is still in the business. In fact, she says she's doing quite well.

Cindy has marketed her theater to attract not only the traditional local family movie crowd, but also the people who live hours away but are nostalgic for the old-time drive-in movie.

One of her friends calls her a master of marketing. Cindy says, "Well, I guess there's some truth to that, but I couldn't sell something I didn't love, and I love this place."

Those who are indecisive about their career and long-term plans are 66 percent less likely to feel that they understand their own identity. (Guerra and Braungart-Rieker 1999)

86

Don't Forget Packaging

We worry about and try to improve our performance all the time. But improving our performance doesn't do us much good if other people fail to realize what we are capable of.

There is a good reason why cereal companies spend more money on advertising than on any other component of their business. Lots of companies make good cereal, but ultimately they sell their product when their good cereal is the one we know of and think of when we're shopping.

Don't forget that in getting what you want, appearance has to complement reality.

JAMES RODRIGUEZ runs a jobs and life skills program called The Next Step in Paterson, New Jersey.

James works with "people who have been forgotten and cast aside, people who have been given up on." He helps get them ready to work and then helps place them.

The Next Step teaches life skills, job skills, and job acquisition skills. "We counsel people on dressing and hygiene and tell them the first impression that you make might be the only chance you get with an employer. It's a delicate issue, but to do justice for the person, we have to touch on it."

It was ironic for James when he realized that while he spent time trying to get people to match their skills to a pleasant presentation, he didn't spend very much time at all on the presentation of The Next Step. "We worried about doing a good job, which is what we are supposed to do, of course. But we didn't worry about looking like we were doing a good job, which is what brings in more grant money and would actually allow us to help more people."

Now James spends more time compiling statistics on the people they've helped and producing reports on the work they do. "It's just like I tell the people I counsel: it's not enough to be right for the job, you've got to look right for the job."

What makes a small business work? Experience, location, and size of staff are important. But no other aspect of the running of small businesses is as predictive of their success as the level of resources they dedicate to marketing. (Goldenberg and Kline 1999)

87

Learn to Lead Yourself

In an ideal world, you would receive the support of everyone you work with, and you would benefit from inspirational leadership provided by your supervisors.

In a practical world, you may find yourself with a supervisor who is more a roadblock to your doing your job than a source of inspiration.

As you grow more certain of your purpose and your talents, however, you will come to rely less on the attitudes and abilities of those around you and more on your own passion and ability.

AFTER TWENTY YEARS in sales, Terry Hinton laments that work "is not a career ladder, it's a career obstacle course. When I've had strong years, they've been written off because I've had a good territory. When I've had lean years, it's as if I'm solely responsible for the company's plight."

While the road to advancement has been blocked, salaries based on commission have provided nicely for Terry. "The reason I've been supported is I've delivered. They've gotten hard work and profitability from me. You can't always get the respect you deserve, but you can still get the paycheck you earned."

The productivity of employees who score high in dedication to their career is 33 percent less likely to be affected by the quality of their managers than is the production of low-dedication employees. (Pollock 1998)

88

A Victory at All Costs Is Not a Victory

Some problems can be avoided more easily than they can be eliminated, and some solutions are more costly than the problems they solve.

In your efforts to be successful, the emphasis must be on winning with a purpose, not merely on winning. Trying to succeed in every single thing you do, winning every disagreement, and getting to do everything your way would lead you to a myopic focus on meaningless confrontations instead of a big-picture focus on what you really want.

KI SUH PARK is one of the leading architects in Los Angeles. He graduated at the top of his class with degrees in architecture and city planning from Berkeley and MIT.

A Korean refugee who came to America during the Korean war, he accepted nothing less than total effort from himself. And he demanded total effort from those around him. He was known for setting records for firing secretaries who had made a mistake, and he raised the hackles of his architectural partners for returning their memos to them with grammatical errors highlighted.

When Los Angeles suffered through the violence and destruction of the riots of 1992, his perspective began to change. Ki Suh was asked to lead Rebuild L.A., an initiative to both replace destroyed buildings and reinvigorate the economy of impoverished sections of Los Angeles.

The experience changed his perspective dramatically. "I used to look through my eyes on everything, form an opinion from my eyes. But I learned that you really have to have empathy for other people, how they see the same thing."

When he took on the project of helping Los Angeles, he was suddenly thrust into thinking about the big picture. "The whole world lives in this city, and if we can make it happen, this can be a model for the future of the entire world."

His purpose has changed—from getting everything done his way to making a contribution to what needs to be done. "I feel like a tiny grain of sand. But you can't remake the world overnight or remake the city overnight. The question is: Are we even taking the first step?"

He gains great satisfaction from working on projects that reflect his vision as well as the wishes of the community. "It is," says Ki Suh, "exhilaration."

The will to succeed comes in two distinct forms. Hypercompetitive people (60 percent) focus on winning all the time, regardless of the importance of the matter. Self-oriented competitive people (40 percent) focus on doing well but with an emphasis on improving themselves so that they can do even better in the future. (Glaman 1999)

89

People Who Have It Right
Work Harder to Make It Better

You might think that people work hard to get something right, and once they do their efforts decrease.

In truth, people who work hard to get something right tend to keep working hard to get it even better.

FOR KAREN ROGERS, the revelation occurred as she implemented an incentive pay program at the property management firm she runs.

An off-par year for the company forced her to seek alternatives to a yearly across-the-board salary increase for her employees. She devised an incentive plan that would be based on a combination of overall profit and personal productivity.

To see what effect the incentives had, she carefully, and for the first time, charted the output of every employee before the plan was announced. "The investment in time was immense, which is the great hidden cost of incentive plans."

When she compared productivity before and after the plan was introduced, she was somewhat surprised to see that nearly one-third of her employees did not increase their output. When she broke the results down further, it became clear that the employees who had not improved were generally the most productive to begin with.

Two years later, when Karen scrapped the incentive plan, she dug out the numbers again. Sure enough, she found a group of workers whose productivity had not meaningfully changed. And it was the same group.

Karen is quick to share what the experience taught her: "The definition of a good employee is someone who already does what you think you might need an incentive plan to get other people to do."

Managers of production facilities who are meeting their quality targets actually invest 20 percent more time in improving their practices than managers of facilities that are falling short of their goals. In other words, the better off work harder to get even better. (Coulthard 1998)

90

Don't Run in the Wrong Direction
Just Because You're Near the Finish Line

How many times do you finish something even though you wish you'd never started it?

We clean our plates even if the carrots are overcooked because they are there and we've already started. We do this even though we would never seek overcooked carrots and wouldn't want them if anyone offered them to us.

We sit in the movie theater and keep watching the movie when we think it's terrible, even though under no circumstances would we say yes if someone asked, "Would you like to watch forty-five minutes of an awful movie?"

We do the same thing when we continue a project that is off target. We keep going because we've already started, not because it makes any sense to continue what we're doing.

Be prepared to stop—based not on what you've already invested but on what you stand to gain by continuing.

BRAD RUNS a high-tech security firm and sees the insides and the decision-making process of all kinds of companies. "The most amazing part of this business is the number of times you'll hear that a business is concerned that their security is inadequate but that they can't make a change right now because they're already paying for another system."

Brad tells them, "Well, if you're already paying for another system that doesn't work, you're not really paying for security."

He adds, "I really question when management teams refuse to make a change, even after they acknowledge the need for it, because they don't want to look bad for having made the wrong decision the first time, or they don't want to waste the money paying twice for something. When I hear that I wonder if they can ever adapt to their environment, or if they will go down in flames because they had to follow the plan no matter what."

In experimental settings, people rate the feasibility of continuing the development of a new product based more on its nearness to completion than on the likelihood of the product producing a profit. (Boehne and Pease 2000)

91

Hope Springs Internal

W̲e look at what's going on around us, and we size up our prospects. Will we make it? We consider the economy and every external factor we can find.

But the best information you have is not national economic reports or even the company newsletter. It is your own approach, and it starts with two simple beliefs: You can get the job done, and you can show others that you can get the job done.

JAMES BLACK WORKED in department stores helping decide which clothes they would sell. But he was convinced he could make better clothes than what his store was selling and that he could make more money doing it.

His co-workers told him it was a long shot and that he should know better than to try.

James was not discouraged and launched jimmy?WEAR in 1995. He worked long hours, and his clothes have steadily gained a foothold in stores across the country.

James has one strategy for persevering in a fashion industry that revolves around intense competition and constant rejection: "No matter what you are trying for, you can't let a no mean no."

Nine in ten people who believe they will one day realize their career goals have strong feelings of competence and assertiveness. (Velting 1999)

92

Think as if Others Can Read Your Mind

A number of science fiction movies have considered the havoc that would be wrought if someone could read minds and hear people's private thoughts.

However, it doesn't take mind-reading for people to accurately perceive others' level of job satisfaction. Your co-workers, your customers, and your family clearly understand, even if you haven't directly said anything, how satisfied and committed you are to your job. Realize that in your tone, demeanor, and body language you are communicating thoughts you have about your job.

MICHAEL PHIPPEN runs a temporary staffing agency in Florida called Staff Leasing. When he took the top job in the company, he spent nearly all his time talking with sales associates. "Nothing begins until you sell something, and they're the first line of folks who know what our customers want, what our customers need, and what we're delivering."

He learned that there was a disconnection between the different groups of the company. Sales and operations were not on the same page, and the customers were lost in the process.

Michael set out to bring everybody together in everything they do. "My success has been in taking disparate areas of the organization with different focuses and bringing them together, to see the common needs of the company and ultimately to create a winning scenario based on all the pieces of the puzzle, not just their focus."

Michael adds, "Once we did that, we began to win those customers back who saw this is really one organization with one purpose."

Co-workers and customers asked to rate the job satisfaction of retail store employees were three times as accurate as random chance. Customers were 70 percent more likely to continue to do business in the store if they found the employees satisfied with their jobs. (Hagan 1999)

93

You'll Get Knocked Down
and Then Get Back Up

So many outcomes seem out of our control. Decisions are made that change our companies, our jobs, our lives—decisions we feel helpless to affect.

But if you can accept some uncertainty and believe in yourself, there will always be alternatives available to you. You will always have a choice no matter what the situation.

AT FIRST the pictures were thrilling, and he called everybody around him to come see. Watching the local evening news, William Morales saw a close-up of a wall he personally had covered with graffiti. Then came the details. William's brother was dying in a local hospital after getting in a shoot-out with police next to that wall.

William sat watching from his jail cell and cried.

And he found a purpose. Over the course of the next few months, another inmate taught him to read. Then William applied to take classes in prison to help him earn a high school degree, and then came job training.

His efforts earned him an early release, and he immediately began looking for ways to help the next generation of young men avoid the kinds of lives both he and his brother had led. William set his sights on a program to bring neighborhood children and police officers together, to forge positive relationships and bring role models into the children's lives.

"When I grew up, I looked up to the drug dealers, the big boys. They were the people who were tangible to me. When I look back at my brother's situation, at my situation, I see that a failure to communicate is what killed him. That's why I dedicate myself to this."

When he's not working with children, William is back hitting the books. He's working on a degree in criminal justice, with an eye toward law school. "I think that'll reinforce my natural advocacy skills. I'd like to take my programs on a larger scale."

When layoffs are announced, everybody is disappointed. But some people are overcome with woe while others are thinking of the next step. Self-image and acceptance of risk accounted for more than half of the reaction of workers who faced significant change in the workplace and were more important than the nature of the changes themselves. (Judge, Thoresen, Pucik, and Welbourne 1999)

94

Keep Your Goals Where You Can See Them

Your goals should be an ever-present part of your life, offering you direction and encouragement.

Don't come up with a list of goals, hide them away somewhere, and check back forty years later to see if you reached them. Create them, use them, follow them, update them, live by them.

CONNIE IS A STUDENT counselor in Milwaukee. She works with high school students to get them thinking about their future and to begin considering possible careers.

"The biggest thing is to get students started. So many of them have no concept of what they might want to do, which means they never consider the things they will have to do to become what they want to be."

Says Connie, "We start talking with them, seriously, to give them a reality check so that they can start formulating their goals.

"Career planning is a lifelong process, but the sooner we start, the better chance we have of making decisions that will benefit us down the line," Connie explains. "Once students have a goal, then they get not only a sense of direction for what they're doing, but also a sense of purpose."

Successful people spend at least fifteen minutes every day thinking about what they are doing and can do to improve their lives. (Sigmund 1999)

95

Don't Settle

People don't buy houses or cars if they're not sure about every detail. It's too important to rush into that kind of commitment.

But how many of us toil in jobs that we don't think are right for us?

You will spend more time between the ages of twenty-five and sixty-five working than you will spend doing anything other than sleeping. Your job not only will define possibilities for your future, it may also come to define you.

Never stop thinking about what you need to do to love what you do.

WILLIAM RASPBERRY is a Pulitzer Prize–winning columnist for the *Washington Post*. He loves his job and wishes more people loved theirs.

"You need to love what you do. Love the hell out of it. Don't settle for just liking your career, for becoming a data processor or school principal or Toyota saleswoman because 'the paycheck's decent and, hey, it's a job.'"

William has a simple test for figuring out if you're in the right line of work: "Imagine the job you have right now paid you the least amount of money you could possibly live on. Would you still want the job? If not, you're not in the right line of work."

Even though they may not want to, people tend to take their jobs home with them at the end of the day. Low levels of career interest are associated with low enjoyment of life overall and even greater dissatisfaction with family life. (O'Brien, Martinez-Pons, and Kopala 1999)

96

What Is the Point?

I f you could pick one thing you most wanted out of your job and your life, what would it be?

While many of us chase money, prestige, and recognition, the single most important thing you can achieve is meaning. Having a purpose in everything you do makes every day valuable and every outcome, good or bad, worthwhile.

BARBARA MILLER is a consultant who studies the workplace and the quality of workers' lives for high-tech companies.

Barbara explains, "The global marketplace is requiring organizations to be open around the clock now, and that is changing both the work and the lives of high-tech employees."

Barbara warns companies that they cannot overlook the strain they place on families when the workday expands or becomes limitless. She reports that many companies talk about work-life balance but then don't practice it. "Just putting in work-life programs isn't going to help people have work-life harmony. We've really got to take a look at the way organizations are structured and change our workplaces accordingly."

Barbara found one organization in which all its engineers were on call every weekend in case of a client emergency. "Anyone could be called away from their families at any time. They could never really relax because they didn't know if they were really off or not. Turnover was very high because many of these people questioned why they would want a job that prevented them from having a life."

Ultimately, Barbara's recommendations were followed, and a new policy was created. In the new schedule, weekend shifts were staffed voluntarily by workers who received weekdays off in return.

Feeling there is meaning in your life is eight times more likely to produce satisfaction than is a high income. (King and Napa 1998)

97

Win Your Own Respect First

You can't make your success contingent on someone else's reaction. Competing to impress your parents, your spouse, your co-workers, or anybody else will ultimately not be fulfilling. You can't conform to their every hope and expectation, and you will experience great frustration when your accomplishments prove insufficient to gain their approval.

If you start with a respect for what you can do that depends on no one else, you will have a much easier time tolerating those for whom nothing is enough.

"IT'S A VICIOUS cycle," reports educator Sally Tucci. Every day she watches inner-city children compete with one another to see who can learn less. "Somewhere along the way they failed, and they became afraid to try. Since they're unwilling to try, they have to make trying the failure and failing the success.

"Students mock anyone who answers a question, who carries their books home at night, who asks a question. The lesson is that if you want to fit in, you better not learn."

Sally tries to break down these attitudes every day. "I say, if your friends tell you up is down and down is up, are you going to listen? You have a chance in this life to do something, but not if you spend your time listening to someone who wants you to do the opposite of the right thing."

Sally attacks the fear as the first step toward building self-confidence. "You have to think about the things you can do instead of the things you can't do—and you'll be amazed at how many things you can do."

Researchers find that an optimistic personal outlook is more than just seeing the bright side of things. Believing in yourself actually produces increases in good health, motivation, and achievement for six in ten people. (Schulman 1999)

98

Your Goals Must Engage All of You

To pursue something difficult you will need commitment, focus, and confidence. You will need the promise of gaining a significant outcome and a sense of fulfillment.

If your goals do not move you, if they do not inspire and incite you to action, then you have not found the right goals.

LACEY BENTON has worked for, and run, a long list of small businesses in the Baltimore area. Unfortunately, after a while she realized her heart wasn't in it. "I could do these jobs, and do them well, but I began to question if they were right for me, if they were what I wanted to do."

While Lacey had enjoyed working with youth groups, she never saw the possibility to make a career out of her efforts. That is, until a community center called the Village Learning Place invited her to oversee its plans to rent out part of its building to create a small café. The rent money would enable the group to expand its programs, and Lacey was asked to help find a suitable tenant.

Then Lacey took their conversation in a whole new direction. "You have teenagers here looking for something worthwhile to do, and you have a space that you'd like to rent to generate some income. Forget about renting it. Let's create a café ourselves," Lacey told the group's board. She proposed letting the teens be involved in every aspect of the operation, while she would use her years of small business experience to make sure it ran smoothly.

With that, Lacey put together a group of teens who learned about the business by visiting other cafés and reading about the subject. The idea of teaching business skills to teens was so intriguing that the center was able to attract grant money to help pay start-up costs of the business. Soon, the Youth Entrepreneur Café, serving coffee and juice, was up and running.

Lacey loves teaching the children about their options in life, that whether they pursue business or something else, "Life is a choice, as opposed to something that happens to them."

As for Lacey, when the mind and heart are focused on the same thing, "I can do anything. Watch me."

When end-of-career managers discussed their relative success and moments of peak performance during their careers, more than half spoke in terms of the significance of personal fulfillment. (Thornton, Privette, and Bundrick 1999)

99

Take Action

Sharks have to keep moving forward to live.

People need to keep moving forward in order for their dreams to live.

You do not need to do everything today, but you do need to do something every day.

MICHAEL FRANKLIN helps make sure everything we order gets to our door on time. He is a vice president for one of American's largest shipping services.

When the company brought in a consulting firm to assess the workplace climate and the leadership skills of executives, many employees were skeptical or even offended. But Michael saw this as an opportunity. "I am past the point of being able to be embarrassed, but if there's something they could point out or teach me that's going to make me a better manager or put me in a better position to advance, then I want to know about it."

The profile that emerged from the consultants noted positively his energy, drive, persistence, and hustle but suggested he could improve his ability to communicate and relate to other employees.

Michael took the report and started scheduling meetings with people above and below him in the company. "I'm very plan focused, so I took what they had to say and immediately tried to put it to use. I think it's made me better at my job already."

Those who do not feel they are taking steps toward their goals are five times more likely to give up and three times less likely to feel satisfied with their lives. (Elliott 1999)

100

Only You Can Say if This Is a World You Can Succeed In

What is the main difference between people who have confidence they will succeed and people who don't? Is it that they live in essentially different worlds—the confident in an easier place where everyone supports their efforts at success and the less confident in a harsher world where it is harder to succeed? No.

The difference is not the world itself. The difference is how they view the world.

The confident construct a reality out of the world around them, a reality in which success is possible because they pay special attention to those who have succeeded and have carefully studied the path to success. Those who lack confidence, meanwhile, pay more attention to those who have failed and the obstacles that exist to thwart their efforts.

It is much like two people walking next to each other on a busy city street, one looking up and the other down. The reality of the city is the same, but the view is very different.

PRIME MINISTER Winston Churchill, who led Great Britain through World War II, is thought of by many experts as perhaps the best example of a person who led a complete life and functioned to the best of all his abilities. Churchill not only led a government through the most overwhelming circumstance, he spent his life engaged in such pursuits as studying, painting, writing, and raising a family.

However, one year after the treaties were signed ending all hostilities in the war, Winston Churchill was voted out of office. He left office shocked and humbled and feeling a failure.

By no reasonable standard would Winston Churchill have to accomplish so much to be considered a success. But at the same time, by only one standard could Winston Churchill consider himself a success. If Churchill did not see himself as having succeeded, then no accomplishment would suffice.

Research on middle-class men from similar backgrounds found that they have greatly divergent views of how difficult it is to succeed economically. Despite the fact that they experienced similar economic and social challenges, some viewed the world as tilted against them, while others saw it as offering great opportunities. The more optimistically they viewed their surroundings, the greater their satisfaction with their job and their confidence in future success. (Franklin and Mizell 1995)

Sources

Alderman, M. K. 1999. *Motivation for Achievement: Possibilities for Teaching and Learning*. Mahwah, NJ: Lawrence Erlbaum Associates.

Arnett, J. 2000. "High Hopes in a Grim World." *Youth and Society* 31:267–86.

Arnold, K. 1995. *Lives of Promise: A Fourteen-Year Study of Achievement and Life Choices*. San Francisco: Jossey-Bass.

Arrison, E. 1998. "Academic Self-Confidence as a Predictor of First-Year College Student Quality of Effort and Achievement." Ph.D. dissertation, Temple University.

Atkinson, S. 1999. "Reflections: Personal Development for Managers." *Journal of Managerial Psychology* 14:502–11.

Austin, L. 2000. *What's Holding You Back?* New York: Basic Books.

Baker, B. 2000. "Responses to Dependence: A Social Exchange Model of Employment Practices in Entrepreneurial Firms." Ph.D. dissertation, University of North Carolina.

Barto, V. 1998. "The Relationship Between Personality Traits of Selected New Jersey Public High School Educators and Successful Academic Achievement of At-Risk Students." Ph.D. dissertation, Seton Hall University.

Bashaw, R. E., and E. S. Grant. 1994. "Exploring the Distinctive Nature of Work Commitments." *Journal of Personal Selling and Sales Management* 14:41–56.

Beadles, N. A., C. Lowery, M. M. Petty, and H. Ezell. 2000. "An Examination of the Relationships Between Turnover Functionality, Turnover Frequency, and Organizational Performance." *Journal of Business and Psychology* 15:331–37.

Black, H. 1999. "A Sense of the Sacred: Altering or Enhancing the Self-Portrait in Older Age?" *Narrative Inquiry* 9:327–45.

Boehne, D., and P. Pease. 2000. "Deciding Whether to Complete or Terminate an Unfinished Project." *Organizational Behavior and Human Decision Processes* 81:178–94.

Boyer, G. 1999. "Turning Points in the Development of Male Servant Leaders." Ph.D. dissertation, Fielding Institute.

Brandes, P. 1998. "Organizational Cynicism: Its Nature, Antecedents, and Consequences." Ph.D. dissertation, University of Cincinnati.

Bridges, C., and V. Perotti. 1993. "Characteristics of Career Achievement: Perceptions of African-American Corporate Executives." *Mid-American Journal of Business* 8:61–64.

Brown, S. 1999. "Holding Up a Mirror: Identity Revision and Its Relationship to Women's Voluntary Career Change." Ph.D. dissertation, Fielding Institute.

Burke, R. 1999. "Managers' Perceptions of Work-Personal Life Balance." *Perceptual and Motor Skills* 89:393–94.

Butler, R. 1999. "Information Seeking and Achievement Motivation in Middle Childhood and Adolescence: The Role of Conceptions of Ability." *Developmental Psychology* 35:146–63.

Bybee, J., S. Luthar, and E. Zigler. 1997. "The Fantasy, Ideal, and Ought Selves." *Social Cognition* 15:37–53.

Byrd, L. 1999. "An Examination of the Relationship Between Personality Types and Career Anchors." Ph.D. dissertation, Walden University.

Carlin, L. 1998. "Becoming Average." Ph.D. dissertation, University of Washington.

Carpenter, S. 2000. "Effects of Cultural Tightness and Collectivism on Self-Concept and Causal Attributions." *Social Science* 34:38–56.

Cassirer, N., and B. Reskin. 2000. "High Hopes: Organizational Position, Employment Experiences, and Women's and Men's Promotion Aspirations." *Work & Occupations* 27:438–63.

Charlton, K. 1999. "Attempting to Gain Access to a High Power Group: The Effects of Boundary Permeability and Outcome." Ph.D. dissertation, University of Missouri.

Chartier, C. T. 1998. "Strategic Leadership: Product and Technology Innovation in High-Technology Companies." Ph.D. dissertation, United States International University.

Childs, B. G. 1998. "Academically Gifted Girls." Ph.D. dissertation, Case Western Reserve University.

Cialdini, R., R. Borden, A. Thorne, M. R. Walker, S. Freeman, and L. R. Sloan. 1999. "Basking in Reflected Glory: Three Field Studies." In *The Self in Social Psychology*, ed. R. Baumeister. Philadelphia: Taylor and Francis.

Comer, L., and T. Drollinger. 1999. "Active Empathetic Listening and Selling Success: A Conceptual Framework." *Journal of Personal Selling and Sales Management* 19:15–29.

Cooper, B., P. Clasen, D. Silva-Jalonen, and M. Butler. 1999. "Creative Performance on an In-Basket Exercise." *Journal of Managerial Psychology* 14:39–56.

Coover, G., and S. Murphy. 2000. "The Communicated Self: Exploring the Interaction Between Self and Social Context." *Human Communication Research* 26:125–47.

Coulthard, P. 1998. "The Quality-Achieving Behavior of Work Group Managers." Ph.D. dissertation, Portland State University.

Craigie, F. 1999. "The Spirit and Work: Observations About Spirituality and Organizational Life." *Journal of Psychology and Christianity* 18:43–53.

Cron, W., E. Jackofsky, and J. Slocum. 1993. "Job Performance and Attitudes of Disengagement Stage Salespeople Who Are About to Retire." *Journal of Personal Selling and Sales Management* 13:1–13.

Dann, A. 1999. "Job Satisfaction and Work Motivation of Connecticut School Superintendents." Ph.D. dissertation, University of Connecticut.

Decker, W., and D. Rotondo. 1999. "Use of Humor at Work: Predictors and Implications." *Psychological Reports* 84:961–68.

Devine, D., L. Clayton, J. Philips, B. Dunford, and S. Melner. 1999. "Teams in Organizations: Prevalence, Characteristics, and Effectiveness." *Small Group Research* 30:678–711.

Dickinson, M. J. 1999. "Do Gooders or Do Betters?" *Educational Research* 41:221–27.

Edley, P. 1998. "Designing Culture: A Feminist Study of Power and Gender in a Woman-Owned and -Operated Interior Design Firm." Ph.D. dissertation, Rutgers University.

Eisenberger, R., L. Rhoades, and J. Cameron. 1999. "Does Pay for Performance Increase or Decrease Perceived Self-Determination and Intrinsic Motivation?" *Journal of Personality and Social Psychology* 77:1026–40.

Elliott, M. 1999. "Time, Work, and Meaning." Ph.D. dissertation, Pacifica Graduate Institute.

Ellis-Payne, R. 1999. "Job Satisfaction and Motivation in the Service Sector." Ph.D. dissertation, Nova Southeastern University.

Elovainio, M., and M. Mivimaeki. 2001. "The Effects of Personal Need for Structure and Occupational Identity in the Role Stress Process." *Journal of Psychology* 141:365–78.

Essic, E. 1999. "The Multiple Mentor Model." Ph.D. dissertation, University of North Carolina at Greensboro.

Evans, K., R. Kleine, T. Landry, and L. Crosby. 2000. "How First Impressions of a Customer Impact Effectiveness in an Initial Sales Encounter." *Journal of the Academy of Marketing Science* 28:512–26.

Fallon, J., J. Avis, J. Kudisch, T. Gornet, and A. Frost. 2000. "Conscientiousness as a Predictor of Productive and Counterproductive Behaviors." *Journal of Business and Psychology* 15:339–49.

Feather, N. T. 1999. "Judgments of Deservingness: Studies in the Psychology of Justice and Achievement." *Personality and Social Psychology Review* 3:86–107.

Fisher, S., W. D. K. Macrosson, and J. Wong. 1998. "Cognitive Style and Team Role Preference." *Journal of Managerial Psychology* 13:544–57.

Flaherty, T., R. Dahlstrom, and S. Skinner. 1999. "Organizational Values and Role Stress as Determinants of Customer-Oriented Selling Performance." *Journal of Personal Selling and Sales Management* 19:1–18.

Franklin, C. W., and C. A. Mizell. 1995. "Some Factors Influencing Success Among African American Men." *Journal of Men's Studies* 3:191–204.

Frome, P. 1999. "The Influence of Girls' Gender-Linked Beliefs on Their Educational and Occupational Aspirations." Ph.D. dissertation, University of Michigan.

Furnham, A., C. Jackson, and T. Miller. 1999. "Personality, Learning Style, and Work Performance." *Personality and Individual Differences* 27:1113–22.

Garver, M. 2000. "Buyer-Salesperson Relationships: Customer Value Created and Delivered by the Salesperson and Its Effect on Customer Satisfaction, Personal Trust, and Personal Loyalty." Ph.D. dissertation, University of Tennessee.

Gerstman, R. 1999. "Multiple Career Identities: The Key to Career Development and Career Transitions of Second Advanced Degree Seekers." Ph.D. dissertation, University of Texas.

Gill, F. 1999. "The Meaning of Work: Lessons from Sociology, Psychology, and Political Theory." *Journal of Socio-Economics* 28:725–43.

Glaman, J. 1999. "Competitiveness and the Similarity-Attraction Effect Among Co-Workers." Ph.D. dissertation, University of Houston.

Goldenberg, S., and T. Kline. 1999. "An Exploratory Study of Predicting Perceived Success and Survival of Small Businesses." *Psychological Reports* 85:365–77.

Goltz, S. 1999. "Can't Stop on a Dime: The Roles of Matching and Momentum in Persistence of Commitment." *Journal of Organizational Behavior Management* 19:37–63.

Gordon, Darlene. 1998. "The Relationship Among Academic Self-Concept, Academic Achievement, and Persistence with Self-Attribution." Ph.D. dissertation, Purdue University Press.

Greene, A. 1999. "Honesty in Organizations: Perceptions of the Corporate Environment and Their Impact on Individual Behavior." Ph.D. dissertation, Brandeis University.

Greno-Malsch, K. L. 1998. "Children's Use of Interpersonal Negotiation Strategies as a Function of their Level of Self-Worth." Ph.D. dissertation, University of Wisconsin, Milwaukee.

Gribble, J. R. 2000. "The Psychosocial Crisis of Industry Versus Inferiority and Self-Estimates of Vocational Competence in High School Students." Ph.D. dissertation, Kent State University.

Guerra, A., and J. Braungart-Rieker. 1999. "Predicting Career Indecision in College Students." *Career Development Quarterly* 47:255–66.

Hagan, C. 1999. "The Relationship Between Employee Job Satisfaction and Key Customer Outcomes." Ph.D. dissertation, Florida Atlantic University.

Harries, C., and N. Harvey. 2000. "Taking Advice, Using Information, and Knowing What You Are Doing." *Acta Psychologica* 104:399–416.

Harrison, Y., and J. Horne. 1999. "One Night of Sleep Loss Impairs Innovative Thinking and Flexible Decision Making." *Organizational Behavior and Human Decision Processes* 78:128–45.

Haugen, R., and T. Lund. 1999. "The Concept of General Expectancy in Various Personality Dispositions." *Scandinavian Journal of Psychology* 40:109–14.

Henderson, E. 1999. "Extensive Engagement: Chief Executive Officers' Formative Life Experiences Related to Their Participative Style of Leadership." Ph.D. dissertation, University of Alberta.

Howatt, W. A. 1999. "Journaling to Self-Evaluation: A Tool for Adult Learners." *International Journal of Reality Therapy* 18:32–34.

Howell, K. 1999. "Coping Strategies and Marital Satisfaction of Dual-Career Couples with Children." Ph.D. dissertation, University of Northern Colorado.

Huffman, C., and L. Cain. 2000. "Effects of Considering Uncontrollable Factors in Sales Force Performance Evaluation." *Psychology and Marketing* 17:799–833.

Ichniowski, C., D. Levine, C. Olsen, and G. Strauss. 2000. *The American Workplace: Skills, Compensation, and Employee Involvement*. New York: Cambridge University Press.

Ingram, M. P. B. 1998. "A Study of Transformative Aspects of Career Change Experiences and Implications for Current Models of Career Development." Ph.D. dissertation, Texas A & M.

Jackson, S., L. Mayocchi, and J. Dover. 1998. "Life After Winning Gold." *Sport Psychologist* 12:137–55.

Johlke, M., D. Duhan, R. Howell, and R. Wilkes. 2000. "An Integrated Model of Sales Managers' Communication Practices." *Journal of the Academy of Marketing Science* 28:263–77.

Johnson, M., T. Beebe, J. Mortimer, and M. Snyder. 1998. "Volunteerism in Adolescence: A Process Perspective." *Journal of Research on Adolescence* 8:309–32.

Jones, D. 2000. "Appreciative Inquiry." Ph.D. dissertation, Benedictine University.

Jones, E., and S. Berglas. 1999. "Control of the Attributions About the Self Through Self-Handicapping Strategies." In *The Self in Social Psychology*, ed. R. Baumeister. Philadelphia: Taylor and Francis.

Judge, T., C. Thoresen, V. Pucik, and T. Welbourne. 1999. "Managerial Coping with Organizational Change." *Journal of Applied Psychology* 84:107–22.

Kang, J., and J. Hillery. 1998. "Older Salespeople's Role in Retail Encounters." *Journal of Personal Selling and Sales Management* 18:39–53.

Kilburg, R. 2000. *Effective Coaching: Developing Managerial Wisdom in a World of Chaos*. Washington, DC: American Psychological Association.

King, L., and C. Napa. 1998. "What Makes a Life Good?" *Journal of Personality and Social Psychology* 75:156–65.

Kisfalvi, V. 2000. "The Threat of Failure, the Perils of Success, and CEO Character: Sources of Strategic Persistence." *Organization Studies* 21:611–39.

Knouse, S., J. Tanner, and E. Harris. 1999. "The Relation of College Internships, College Performance, and Subsequent Job Opportunity." *Journal of Employment Counseling* 36:35–43.

Knowles, P., S. Grove, and K. Keck. 1994. "Signal Detection Theory and Sales Effectiveness." *Journal of Personal Selling and Sales Management* 14:1–14.

Layman, P. 1999. "An Investigation into the Relationship Between Perceived and Observed Group Development Patterns of Corporate Work and Project Teams." Ph.D. dissertation, Temple University.

Lockwood, P., and Z. Kunda. 2000. "Outstanding Role Models: Do They Inspire or Demoralize Us?" In *Psychological Perspectives on Self and Identity,* ed. A. Tesser. Washington, DC: American Psychological Association.

Lucas, M. 1999. "Adult Career Changers." *Journal of Employment Counseling* 36:115–18.

Lusnar, M. 1999. "Job Applicant Stereotypes: Effects of Eyeglasses and Job Type in a Simulated Interview." Ph.D. dissertation, Loyola University.

Maasen, G., and J. Landsheer. 2000. "Peer-Perceived Social Competence and Academic Achievement of Low-Level Educated Young Adolescents." *Social Behavior and Personality* 28:29–40.

MacGregor, J., T. Ormerod, and E. Chronicle. 1999. "Spatial and Contextual Factors in Human Performance on the Traveling Salesperson Problem." *Perception* 28:1417–27.

MacKenzie, S., P. Podsakoff, and J. Paine. 1999. "Do Citizenship Behaviors Matter More for Managers than for Salespeople?" *Journal of the Academy of Marketing Science* 27:396–410.

Maddock, R. 2000. *Motigraphics: The Analysis and Measurement of Human Motivations in Marketing.* Westport, CT: Quorum Books.

Markman, K., and P. Tetlock. 2000. "'I Couldn't Have Known': Accountability, Forseeability, and Counterfactual Denials of Responsibility." *British Journal of Social Psychology* 39:313–25.

Marshall, G., and J. Mowen. 1993. "An Experimental Investigation of the Outcome Bias in Salesperson Performance Evaluations." *Journal of Personal Selling and Sales Management* 13:31–47.

Marshall, G., M. Stamps, and J. Moore. 1998. "Preinterview Biases: The Impact of Race, Physical Attractiveness, and Sales Job Type on Preinterview Impressions of Sales Job Applicants." *Journal of Personal Selling and Sales Management* 18:21–38.

Mathieu, A. 1998. "An Expanded Turnover Model: Examination of the Mediating Role of Three Coping Strategies on the Job Stress-Anxiety Relationship." Ph.D. dissertation, University of Cincinnati.

Mayo, M. W., and N. Christenfeld. 1999. "Gender, Race, and Performance Expectations of College Students." *Journal of Multicultural Counseling and Development* 27:93–104.

McCaw, W. 1999. "The Perception of Followers." Ph.D. dissertation, University of Montana.

McGregor, I. D. 1999. "An Identity Consolidation View of Social Phenomena: Theory and Research." Ph.D. dissertation, University of Waterloo.

McIntyre, R., R. Claxton, K. Anselmi, and E. Wheatley. 2000. "Cognitive Style as an Antecedent to Adaptiveness, Customer Orientation, and Self-Perceived Selling Performance." *Journal of Business and Psychology* 15:179–96.

Melnarik, C. 1999. "Retaining High Tech Employees." Ph.D. dissertation, Walden University.

Mendoza, J. C. 1999. "Resiliency Factors in High School Students at Risk for Academic Failure." Ph.D. dissertation, California School of Professional Psychology.

Moeller, J., and O. Koeller. 2000. "Spontaneous and Reactive Attributions Following Academic Achievement." *Social Psychology of Education* 4:67–86.

Moncrief, W., E. Babakus, D. Cravens, and M. Johnston. 2000. "Examining Gender Differences in Field Sales Organizations." *Journal of Business Research* 49:245–57.

Moore, C. 1999. "Understanding Voluntary Employee Turnover Within the New Workplace Paradigm: A Test of an Integrated Model." Ph.D. dissertation, Claremont Graduate University.

Morris, M., R. LaForge, and J. Allen. 1994. "Salesperson Failure." *Journal of Personal Selling and Sales Management* 14:1–15.

Morrow, M., and W. Wurtz. 2000. "Measuring the Impact Resulting from Implementing an Organizational Capability Plan." *Organization Development Journal* 18:65–74.

Mount, M., M. Barrick, and J. Strauss. 1999. "The Joint Relationship of Conscientiousness and Ability with Performance: Test of the Interaction Hypothesis." *Journal of Management* 25:707–21.

Nolan, T. 1999. "The Effects of a Combination of Feedback, Goals, and Consequences on the Performance of Four Small Businesses." Ph.D. dissertation, Western Michigan University.

O'Brien, V., M. Martinez-Pons, and M. Kopala. 1999. "Mathematics Self-Efficacy, Ethnic Identity, Gender, and Career Interests Related to Mathematics and Science." *Journal of Educational Research* 92:231–35.

Orlick, T. 1998. *Embracing Your Potential*. Champaign, IL: Human Kinetics.

Orrange, R. 1999. "Defining One's Life Plans for Work, Family, and Leisure: The Case of Law and MBA Students." Ph.D. dissertation, University of Texas.

Pablo, A. 1999. "Managerial Risk Interpretations." *Journal of Managerial Psychology* 14:92–107.

Parks, C. 1999. "Personality and the Prediction of Turnover of Insurance Sales Agents." Ph.D. dissertation, University of Sarasota.

Patrick, J. 1996. "Age and Expertise Effects on Decision-Making Processes and Outcomes." Ph.D. dissertation, University of Akron.

Pauk, W. 1997. *How to Study in College*. Boston: Houghton Mifflin.

Peiperl, M., and Y. Baruch. 1997. "Back to Square Zero: The Post-Corporate Career." *Organizational Dynamics* 25:7–22.

Persley, R. 1998. "Towards a New Understanding of Organizational Behavior, Sport, and Peak Performance Phenomena." Ph.D. dissertation, Union Institute.

Peterson, R., M. Cannito, and S. Brown. 1995. "An Exploratory Investigation of Voice Characteristics and Selling Effectiveness." *Journal of Personal Selling and Sales Management* 15:1–15.

Pitt, L., P. Berthon, and M. Robson. 2000. "Communication Apprehension and Perceptions of Salesperson Performance." *Journal of Managerial Psychology* 15:68–86.

Polivy, J., and C. P. Herman. 1999. "The Effects of Resolving to Diet on Restrained and Unrestrained Eaters." *International Journal of Eating Disorders* 26:434–47.

———. 2000. "The False-Hope Syndrome: Unfulfilled Expectations of Self-Change." *Current Directions in Psychological Science* 9:128–31.

Pollock, K. 1998. "The Relationship Between Leadership Style and Subordinate Satisfaction and Performance in Public Accounting Firms." Ph.D. dissertation, University of Kentucky.

Quinn, K., N. Roese, G. Pennington, and J. Olson. 1999. "The Personal/Group Discrimination Discrepancy: The Role of Informational Complexity." *Personality and Social Psychology Bulletin* 25:1430–40.

Ricaurte, R. A. 1999. "Student Success in a Communicative Classroom: A Grounded Theory." Ph.D. dissertation, University of Nebraska.

Roberts, B., and W. Friend. 1998. "Career Momentum in Midlife Women." *Journal of Occupational Health Psychology* 3:195–208.

Robeson, R. 1998. "College Students on the Rebound." Ph.D. dissertation, Indiana University.

Russ, F., K. McNeilly, and J. Comer. 1996. "Leadership, Decision Making, and Performance of Sales Managers." *Journal of Personal Selling and Sales Management* 16:1–15.

Sand, G. 1998. "Social Support Networks and Coping Resources Decrease Burnout Levels in Boundary Spanners." Ph.D. dissertation, Nova Southeastern University.

Scamehorn, R. 1990. "The Challenge of Negotiations." *Mid-American Journal of Business* 5:9–12.

Scherneck, M. 1998. "The Relationship Between Self-Esteem and Academic Performance." Ph.D. dissertation, State University of New York at Albany.

Schoonover, J. 1999. "Leadership Characteristics Enabling Corporate Transformations." Ph.D. dissertation, Union Institute.

Schulman, P. 1999. "Applying Learned Optimism to Increase Sales Productivity." *Journal of Personal Selling and Sales Management* 19:31–37.

Schulz, E. 1998. "The Influence of Group Incentives, Training, and Other Human Resource Practices on Firm Performance and Productivity." Ph.D. dissertation, Rutgers University.

Schwer, R. K., and R. Daneshvary. 2000. "Keeping Up One's Appearance: Its Importance and the Choice of Type of Hair-Grooming Establishment." *Journal of Economic Psychology* 21:207–22.

Sedlacek, W. 1999. "Black Students on White Campuses." *Journal of College Student Development* 40:538–50.

Shepard, C. D., and L. Fine. 1994. "Role Conflict and Role Ambiguity Reconsidered." *Journal of Personal Selling and Sales Management* 14:57–65.

Sigmund, E. 1999. "Consciously Directing the Creative Process in Business." *Transactional Analysis Journal* 29:222–27.

Silverman, L. 1998. "Through the Lens of Giftedness." *Roeper Review* 20:204–10.

Smith, A. 2000. "Understanding the Impact of the Founder's Legacy in Current Organizational Behavior." In *Dynamic Consultation in a Changing Workplace,* ed. E. Klein. Madison, CT: Psychosocial Press.

Soellner, A. 1999. "Asymmetrical Commitment in Business Relationships." *Journal of Business Research* 46:219–33.

Sojka, J., A. Gupta, and T. Hartman. 2000. "Student Perceptions of Sales Careers: Implications for Educators and Recruiters." *Mid-American Journal of Business* 15:55–63.

Sparkes, A. 1998. "Athletic Identity: An Achilles' Heel to the Survival of Self." *Qualitative Health Research* 8:644–64.

Sparrow, K. R. 1998. "Resiliency and Vulnerability in Girls During Cognitively Challenging Tasks." Ph.D. dissertation, Florida State University, Tallahassee.

Spiller, M. 1999. "Does Time Heal All Wounds? A Longitudinal Examination of the Joint and Separate Effects of Attribution and Emotion on Self-Efficacy." Ph.D. dissertation, University of Alabama.

Stanek, S. 1998. "The Impact of Extrinsic Rewards of Adult Learning Performance in Independent Study." Ph.D. dissertation, University of Minnesota.

Stanton, H. 1998. "Executive Decisiveness and the Serenity Place." *Australian Journal of Clinical and Experimental Hypnosis* 26:157–64.

Sternberg, R., G. Forsythe, J. Hedlund, J. Horvath, R. Wagner, W. Williams, S. Snook, and E. Grigorenko. 2000. *Practical Intelligence in Everyday Life.* New York: Cambridge University Press.

Stone, W. 1999. "The Relationship Between CEOs' Functional Experience Orientation and Firm Performance, Moderated by Perceived Environmental Uncertainty." Ph.D. dissertation, Virginia Commonwealth University.

Sundvik, L., and M. Lindeman. 1998. "Performance Rating Accuracy: Convergence Between Supervisor Assessment and Sales Productivity." *International Journal of Selection and Assessment* 6:9–15.

Szinovacz, M., and S. DeViney. 1999. "The Retiree Identity." *Journal of Gerontology* 54:207–18.

Tellesfsen, T. 1999. "The Impact of Intra-Organizational Behavior on Inter-Organizational Relationships." Ph.D. dissertation, City University of New York.

Thornton, F., G. Privette, and C. Bundrick. 1999. "Peak Performance of Business Leaders: An Experience Parallel to Self-Actualization Theory." *Journal of Business and Psychology* 14:253–64.

Trope, Y., and E. Pomerantz. 1998. "Resolving Conflicts Among Self-Evaluative Motives." *Motivation and Emotion* 22:53–72.

Tuuli, P., and S. Karisalmi. 1999. "Impact of Working Life Quality on Burnout." *Experimental Aging Research* 25:441–49.

Van Breda, A. 1999. "Developing Resilience to Routine Separations." *Families in Society* 80:597–605.

Velting, D. 1999. "Personality and Negative Expectations: Trait Structure of the Beck Hopelessness Scale." *Personality and Individual Differences* 26:913–21.

Verbeke, W., and R. Bagozzi. 2000. "Sales Call Anxiety: Exploring What It Means When Fear Rules a Sales Encounter." *Journal of Marketing* 64:88–101.

Verive, J. 1997. "The Role of Personality in Personnel Psychology: Using a Typology to Select Sales People." Ph.D. dissertation, University of Akron.

Viveiros, G. 1999. "An Investigation into the Relationship Between Effective Teams and Individual Team Member Behavior Patterns." Ph.D. dissertation, University of Colorado.

Voss, G., and Z. Voss. 2000. "Strategic Orientation and Firm Performance in an Artistic Environment." *Journal of Marketing* 64:67–83.

Werneck De Almeida, E. S. 1999. "Social Integration and Academic Confidence." Ph.D. dissertation, University of Hartford.

Whatley, A. 1998. "Gifted Women and Teaching: A Compatible Choice?" *Roeper Review* 21:117–24.

Wiesenfeld, B., S. Raghuram, and G. Raghu. 1999. "Managers in a Virtual Context." In *Trends in Organizational Behavior,* ed. C. Cooper. New York: Wiley and Sons.

Williams, E., E. Soeprapto, K. Like, P. Touradji, S. Hess, and C. Hill. 1998. "Perceptions of Serendipity." *Journal of Counseling Psychology* 45:379–89.

Williams, R., and L. Matthewman. 1999. "Top Managers in Local Government: Influences on Development." *Journal of Managerial Psychology* 14:69–78.

Wotruba, T., and S. Castleberry. 1993. "Job Analysis and Hiring Practices for National Account Marketing Positions." *Journal of Personal Selling and Sales Management* 13:49–65.

Wright, B. 2000. "An Empirical Examination of the Outcome Effects of Downsizing on Decision Makers." Ph.D. dissertation, Queen's University.

Zeidner, M., and E. J. Schleyer. 1999. "The Big Fish Little Pond Effect for Academic Self-Concept, Test Anxiety, and School Grades in Gifted Children." *Contemporary Educational Psychology* 24:305–29.

Acknowledgments

I offer my sincere appreciation to Gideon Weil, my editor, for his guidance and encouragement, and to Sandy Choron, my agent, for her boundless enthusiasm and dedication. My great thanks are also due to the staff of Harper San Francisco for their skilled assistance in this work.